# The World of Fairy Tales:
## A path to the essence of the young child through fairy tales

Daniel Udo de Haes

*The World of Fairy Tales: A path to the essence of the young child through fairy tales*

First English Edition © 2017 Waldorf Early Childhood Association of North America

ISBN: 978-1-936849-43-7

Author: Daniel Udo de Haes
Translator: Barbara Mees
Copy Editor: Bill Day
Publications Coordinator: Donna Lee Miele
Graphic Design: Amy Thesing
Cover Image: Arthur Rackham, "The Frog Prince," 1909

Originally published in Dutch as *Kleuterwereld-sprookjeswereld* by Vrij geestesleven, Zeist, Netherlands

Published in the United States by the Waldorf Early Childhood Association of North America
285 Hungry Hollow Road Spring Valley, NY 10977
www.waldorfearlychildhood.org
Visit our online store at **store.waldorfearlychildhood.org**

This publication is made possible through a grant from the Waldorf Curriculum Fund.

*A golden thread runs through the fabric of old folk tales. We find the human being and humanity in the world of fairy tales.*

Daniel Udo de Haes (1899-1986)

# Contents

**1 | Why do we tell fairy tales to young children? ..................... 7**
The human being and humanity in the world of fairy tales .......................... 9
Figures .......................................................................................... 18
"Sleeping Beauty": a fairy tale about the fall of man and salvation ............... 21
"Mother Holle": the conscious world and the dream world.......................... 25

**2 | The world of the young child ....................................... 33**
How do young children experience their surroundings? ............................ 33
Children who reject fairy tales ......................................................... 38
Clutter.......................................................................................... 39
The young child and crafts............................................................... 42
Ordinary things.............................................................................. 43

**3 | A few more thoughts on early childhood and fairy tales.... 51**
Why metaphors and not concepts? ...................................................... 51
The cabbage and the stork ................................................................ 53
"Cruelty" and other alarming aspects of fairy tales ................................ 56
About morals in fairy tales and fables .................................................. 59

**4 | Some tips for telling fairy tales ...................................... 65**
The prince in animal form.................................................................. 68
"The Donkey" (Wilhelm Grimm) ............................................................ 68
"The Frog Prince" or "Iron Henry" (Jacob Grimm).................................. 80
The "three sisters and three brothers" motif ........................................ 94

**5 | How to choose and tell fairy tales.................................109**
"Life fairy tales".............................................................................109
Fairy tales and the temperaments.......................................................111
How do we tell different fairy tales for specific temperaments? ..................113
How many fairy tales is enough?.........................................................114
The craving for "new" and "true" stories...............................................115
For the youngest children: what about happy endings? ...........................119
Fairy tales for older children.............................................................122
Preparing to tell fairy tales................................................................123
Sounds carry the content...................................................................125
Refrain from explaining the stories......................................................126
Refrain from preaching.....................................................................127
Choosing illustrated fairy tales...........................................................128
Dare to make mistakes.....................................................................130

**6 | Afterword ...............................................................133**

**About the Author ..........................................................137**

# 1 | Why do we tell fairy tales to young children?

Are fairy tales good for young children?

This question was meaningless in centuries past, when telling fairy tales to young children was the most normal thing in the world. As people became more and more sober-minded and materialistic, they began to see fairy tales as falsehoods. Even Dr. Maria Montessori forbade the telling of these "lies" to children—at first. Thus, we should ask ourselves: "Should we tell fairy tales to young children, and, if so, why?"

In order to find an answer to this question we must first learn to understand the essence of the young child and also learn to see what fairy tales actually tell us. We would first like to try to answer the last question, and will return to the first question later on.

Proverbs and sayings speak to us in a language similar to the language of fairy tales. They can help us learn to understand the contents of these stories. For example, if someone says: "Still waters run deep," someone else, who only thinks extraneously, will not agree: still waters are not deep at all, sometimes even very shallow, while wildly moving seas can be immensely deep. The person who understands the metaphor will appreciate that the saying refers to mankind and should not be seen literally, but figuratively, as describing a truth about the essence of humanity.

Fairy tales speak to us in the same manner. Literally speaking, the things they tell us are often impossible. However, in the form of *images* they express deep and great truths. The difference between proverbs or sayings and fairy tales is that the former talk to us about life as we know and understand it, while the fairy tale goes so deep that its truths are not easily understood, not even by adults. So why does it make sense to tell young children fairy tales?

The next example helps us to take the step from proverbs to fairy tales by bringing us to underlying motifs. Everyone knows the proverb: "Every cloud has a silver lining." We can translate this in a way that everyone will understand: one should not worry too much if one encounters adversity or difficulties; every bad situation has an element of good. Good times will return!

But this proverb can also be seen in a wider context. Clouds are a creation of the sun itself. Without the sun, there would be no clouds and without clouds the sun could not be felt as a blessing (think of life in the desert). Light and darkness are inseparable. The true essence of light can only be experienced after having gone through darkness. Behind the clouds, the light shines, light that has created the clouds and that can only reveal itself in all its splendor through darkness.

If we search for the relationship between light and darkness in the world of legends, we might think of the story of Job in the Old Testament. This story tells us how God allowed Satan to test Job. Satan induced Job to go through the most horrible experiences ("darkness"). Not until he had endured the darkness could he find light in his life. Only then could he become a full servant of God. This image is also found in the Book of Jonah. Jonah could not accomplish his task until he had been "swallowed" by the "big fish" (oncoming Christianity that first put him to the test) and had returned to see the world as a prophet (i.e., initiated in the spirit; Jonah 1:15-3:5)

## The human being and humanity in the world of fairy tales

Now the step to the world of fairy tales is only a small one. Aren't Little Red Riding Hood and her Grandmother swallowed up by the wolf only to return reborn from the darkness? Rebirth is not emphasized in this fairy tale, but the young child will certainly feel it. Here, as in the stories of Job and Jonah, we can see how disappearing and returning from the darkness is a large and essential experience in the development of mankind.

Of course, a young child cannot understand this when listening to the story of Little Red Riding Hood, but he takes the images of the fairy tale into his childish susceptibility as seeds in his soul. These seeds will grow and later, when thinking skills are developed in the soul of the child, they will blossom to form understandable thoughts. Thoughts that surface in this way, that grow from inner planted seeds, are endlessly richer and deeper than those that come to mankind from the intellectual outside. Here lies the main reason why fairy tales should be heard in early childhood. We will come back to this.

The fact that the sun creates the clouds that obscure it is also found in a somewhat different form in the fairy tale "The Tree and the Axe" by Rudolf Steiner. In short, when the axe tells the tree that it is going to chop the tree down, the tree reminds the axe that the axe has received its handle from a *tree*. We adults also take in such images, even though we may not be able to understand the deeper meaning. However, if we walk around with these questions in our subconscious, we may one day find that they have created new possibilities in our thought process.

"The Snow Queen" by Hans Christian Andersen sheds a strange light on the relationship between good and evil, between light and darkness, in the world of children's fairy tales. In this tale, little Kay gets a crystal splinter in his eye that makes him see only the bad and ugly in everything. The whole crystal could be seen as an image for the clear, fair world order. Through his understanding of the world, modern man only sees a small splinter of this crystal. He has gotten a crystal splinter—a limited understanding of the world—in his eye and therefore has a limited conception of the world. In short: human knowledge has become more and more a sharp splinter of the previously common, all-encompassing wisdom. This sharp splinter cuts and wounds everything around it.

This same fact is clarified even further in the Bible, in which we are told how humanity came into darkness because Adam and Eve ate from the Tree of Knowledge of Good and Evil (Genesis 3:6).

It may feel strange that acquiring knowledge of good and evil is seen as a sin (Genesis 2:17), especially when it is seen as the first and most fundamental sin of mankind, a sin that brought darkness to the world. We will try and find a connection to this subject, as it is the main theme of the entire world of fairy tales.

Spiritual science, as presented by Rudolf Steiner, shows us how ancient humanity lived before the fall of man, when it was still immersed in a deep, dreaming connection with its spiritual origins. Mankind still lived completely in God and everything on earth was "good," although "good" as the opposite of "evil" was not yet known because there was no evil. Thus, the duality of "good and evil" was as yet unborn.

Pure mankind that still lived in the glory of God before the Fall is introduced to us in the Bible as a solitary couple, living in paradise and walking and speaking with God. Then the snake comes and offers Eve (the dreamy feminine aspect of humanity) the fruit of the Tree of Knowledge of Good and Evil. By accepting this "knowledge fruit," humanity receives consciousness *apart from* God. In other words, by receiving a new consciousness apart from God, humanity was placed in opposition to the trustworthy spiritual world.

The Oberufer Paradise Play emphasizes the snake's act of *picking* the apple, because through that deed the fruit of knowledge is detached from its divine origins. Human knowledge became a fruit detached from the divine world.[1]

We should not suppose that knowledge, given to mankind by the Tree of Knowledge, was "something evil." "Something evil" did not yet exist, and the possibility to understand it even less so. It was *self-knowledge*, a personal *consciousness* that broke the tie with God. Up until now, mankind had only lived and acted through inspiration from God: we were not able to do anything on our own. Self-knowledge gave us the beginnings of independence, standing on our own facing God. But by standing across from God, mankind became alienated from God. We must have felt abandoned by Him, or, as the Bible says: we now saw that we were "naked": we had lost God's sheath, God's loving protection. This alienation was the first "sin," the Fall of Mankind; mankind "detached" itself from God.

The independence that mankind received through this first separation from God also brought the first sense of freedom. Before the Fall, mankind *could not* do other than walk guided by God wherever God wanted. Human beings slowly became capable of acting out of individual knowledge, individual consciousness. Then arose questions: "What should I do, what shouldn't I do?" "What brings me back to God and what distances me further from Him?" "What is good and what is not good?" Mankind first learned to distinguish between "good and evil." Thus, we can understand that the Bible calls the forbidden tree the "Tree of Knowledge of Good and Evil."

In order to understand this more clearly, we can think of a small-scale example that we can witness time and time again: the development of the child. Later we will return to how large-scale world developments are repeated on a small scale. In the life of every small child, we find a reflection of this drama that is called the "Fall of Man" in Biblical terms.

Like mankind before the Fall, in her first phase of life the small child lives in a deep, dreamlike connection with the divine world, from where her soul has come. She does not yet understand or know earthly things or interrelationships. She still lives half in heaven, or the spiritual world; we could say, she is still in "Paradise." The first, earthly knowledge that is developed, in other words the first, dreamy understanding that is reached, is accompanied by an incipient, progressive loss of innocence. The child begins to be conscious of herself and thus also learns the difference between "good and evil." She learns (not through words but through feelings) the difference between what harmonizes with the world order that has carried her thus far and those things that distance her, that remove her from this same world order. The dreamy protection that she had in her divine origins is lost, leading to an awakening consciousness of her surroundings in her ninth to tenth years. We can again say: through the acquisition of knowledge, self-consciousness, the child is "detached" from her heavenly Being. This development continues for a number of years, until the personal, awakened "I" leads this independence into honest, self-chosen paths.

In the larger development of mankind, the Fall did not occur at once. It is an event that has been taking place for thousands of years. It is still happening and will continue to happen for centuries to come. The enormous drama of mankind continues its development, creating an ever-greater distance from God and from the spiritual origins of our existence.

This would have fatal consequences for mankind if a solution were not pursued simultaneously. The center of this pursuit, which has always had a deep spiritual and divine origin, has manifested itself in changing forms corresponding to the development of mankind through the centuries. The great mysteries and ancient cultures can be seen as the fruits of this spiritually inspired goal of mankind.

In our time, we can also see this pursuit, especially in today's phase of the evolution of humanity. However, modern humanity's way of thinking has become so materialistic that we will not or will hardly recognize the designated intention. Only through a profound spiritual involvement in our true essence will mankind, even in today's phase of evolution, be able to find a closer connection to our task, a task that has grown out of world events. Trying to find a solution to the Fall, which stems from the spiritual world, not only reveals itself in the ancient mysteries, but also in the spiritual science, or anthroposophy, conceptualized by Rudolf Steiner. This science endeavors to make the resurrection of Christ amongst humanity a reality. This book, through this science, tries to find part of the abovementioned connection through examining the essence of the young child and the world of fairy tales.

We just discussed how all the events surrounding the Fall are repeated in the life of a young child. If this truth is to be fully understood, it will become clear that a child's soul and its true development cannot be understood unless one simultaneously searches for an intimate bond with the ancient drama of mankind. We will also begin to understand how this immense drama (which has its resolution in the future) is woven like a golden thread through all the important folk tales that originated in the childhood years of humanity. If we look at all of this together, we will see that a deeper understanding of the young child lies in understanding the trinity of the child, the fairy tale, and the Fall of Mankind as a unity. In much the same way, in order to understand the Fall or fairy tales, the essence of the young child must first be investigated. Since the aim of this book is to arrive at a deeper understanding of the relationship between children and fairy tales, it will only be natural that we should also try to understand something of the Fall of Mankind as well as its solution for the future.

As the urge for general knowledge is becoming more and more materialistic in our time, the separation of mankind from its divine origins is rapidly increasing. For us, and for the people around us, it is difficult to fathom this negative side to our insatiable thirst for knowledge. We admire the power of modern science. The good that it accomplishes should not be underestimated. However, the fact that it also threatens our species with eventual ruin (think of modern warfare) must open our eyes to the large role that materialism and egocentricity play in our pursuit of knowledge.

It is impossible for us to ignore the increasing significance of the negative side to our urgency for knowledge by just avoiding science in general. Some people, especially those who are inclined to Eastern philosophies, do just this. By dismissing modern knowledge, our connection with God is not re-established and we will not get anywhere, which is even worse. It is better that we try to develop the knowledge and internalize it in such a way that it reopens our hearts to the world and to those around us. Thus, the fall of Adam, who seized the fruit of egotistical knowledge, will not be undone but will be *healed* by using this knowledge for the love that Christ placed in our hearts. The common belief that "knowledge is power" will eventually destroy us; it must be supplanted by the motto spoken by Ernest Lehrs: "Knowledge nurtures love" ("Erkenntnis nährt Liebe"). Only this belief can bring us back into the light, out of the darkness that knowledge has brought us. The small, sharp splinter of our intellect can be cut into a new jewel that once again lets the light shine in all directions.

As mentioned above, the drama of mankind that is observed in each individual life can also be seen in another way: Humanity became disobedient to God. Every child becomes disobedient to his parents at some point in his development. If we understand this, we will not suppress it but will lead the child's disobedience to healthy independence. In much the same way, mankind's disobedience to God will eventually develop his spiritual, independent cooperation in world evolution. Each person must follow the same path of development as all of mankind and must also aim for the same ideal.

The mirroring of mankind in each human being can also be seen the other way around in fairy tales. That is to say: everything that is said about a single character in the tale also has meaning for the entire world. Not only was Little Red Riding Hood engulfed by darkness (the wolf) to then return to the light, but every human soul, all mankind, threw itself into the darkness of the Fall, only to find new light through the power of Christ.

Light and darkness can be found in many other fairy tales. Tom Thumb must leave his "Fatherly home" together with his brothers and enter the dark forest to find his Father (that is, the "world Father") again after many adventures. Snow White must rise from the dead to be able to marry her prince and become queen. Sleeping Beauty sleeps for one hundred years, and although the spell should have caused her death, she is awakened by the prince. The Seven Little Goats are swallowed by the wolf, just like Little Red Riding Hood, and then freed from the dark stomach. Thus, we see many fairy tales describe the loss of the Fatherly world of light, entering the darkness, and finally escaping the darkness to once again enter the light. In other words, we see how fairy tales create a representation of the great drama of mankind in a way that appeals to the soul of young children. Fairy tales include a finale. The Bible gives us the same message but in entirely different images and the New Testament shows us the way to achieve the finale. This is the brilliant golden thread of the development of mankind that is woven through the multicolored tapestry of old folk tales.

Finally, let's not forget how close the smallest child is to her pre-birth (divine) origins and, in her deeply dreamy state, how interwoven she still is with the developmental drama of mankind. She must have an inner premonition that she must experience this Fall in her own life in her own small way and will have to try and conquer it. Seen in this light, it should be obvious why young children are endlessly intrigued by the old (unchanged) folk tales and why they cannot get enough of them.

We should also be able to understand that these folk tales, which depict the descent into and the victory over darkness and the path towards new light, give an enormous amount of support to children throughout their lives. This is especially true for children who are older and have "forgotten" the tales. The tales have then had a chance to leave consciousness and sink deeper into the child's soul. We will return to this subject later on. Thus, we arrive at the first and probably most important reason why it is good to tell young children fairy tales: fairy tales subconsciously connect the young child, and also us, to the great development of mankind and in this way make us all real citizens of the earth. Each fairy tale is a small bible in its own way—Old and New Testament together—painted in colors that appeal to the young child. Fairy tales are what we can call a little "Early Childhood Bible."

We would now like to go into the fairy tales that we mentioned earlier. Let's first take a look at "Little Red Riding Hood." This fairy tale clearly and dramatically paints the image of the descent into darkness and return to the light.

Aside from that, we also see other elements of the story of the Fall. The prologue, which is described as the temptation by the snake and disobedience of man to God (Genesis 3:1-7), is also described in "Little Red Riding Hood," although much more subtly. It is described in the conversation between Little Red Riding Hood and the wolf. The evil animal lures the human soul (personified in Little Red Riding Hood) to pick the flowers around her. This image looks just as innocent as picking the apple from the Tree of Knowledge. However, we actually see how being a servant of God (the warning by the mother) is discarded for personal sense perception. *Consciously* enjoying the flowers, something that can be so good for us, was in its origins first seen as a separation from God. We can still find this when looking at the development of mankind. Little children cannot consciously enjoy something yet. They live *intensely* in the world of color, form, tone, etc. They cannot *consciously* admire these things yet. As soon as consciousness for something such as beauty is reached, part of the natural, dreamy connection with the world of the Father is lost. A certain distance is created that allows the first conscious observations to be experienced. The child experiences the beginnings of a kind of "Fall." Little Red Riding Hood experiences this as a certain disobedience: she was told not to listen to the wolf, but she did so anyway; he makes her conscious of the beauty of the flowers. She picks them and is consequently consumed by darkness as she temporarily disappears into the stomach of the wolf.

The Fall of Mankind is also clearly seen in "Snow White"; as in the Bible, the fruit of temptation is an apple (figure 1). The astonishing thing is that this wholesome fruit, so full of nourishment, tempted mankind to evil. But let's remember this: what was originally seen as *evil*, the independence that man wanted from God and that distanced him from God, does not have to be evil and can even grow into something good if it absorbs the impulse of Christ, who approached the world with love. The apple is a crisp fruit that awakens us and gives us strength for independence through its iron element. We can no longer do without those original "sins." We need the strength and independence that they have brought us in order to make the love of Christ into a reality on earth.[2]

Even the world of numbers reveals the duality of the apple as described above. Let's compare the numbers six and five. The well-balanced, harmonious, equally divisible number six can be seen as coming from the cosmos. The circle is a geometric image of the cosmos. The radius can be placed on the circumference six

Fig. 1

Which number did the stepmother offer Snow White?

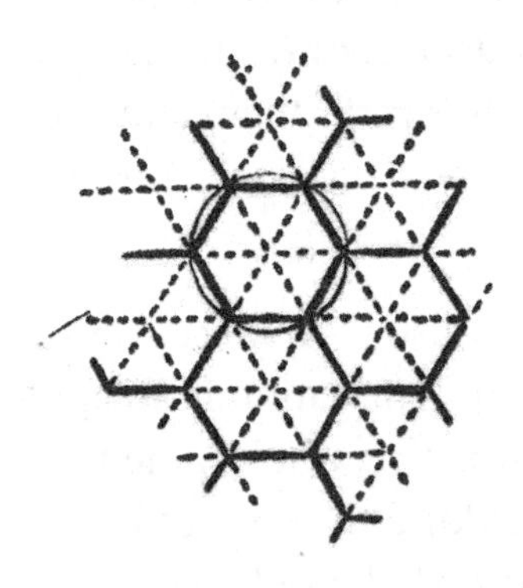

Fig. 2

Where is the clear honey kept by the bees?
In the pure six-sided honeycomb cells.

Fig. 3

Fig. 4

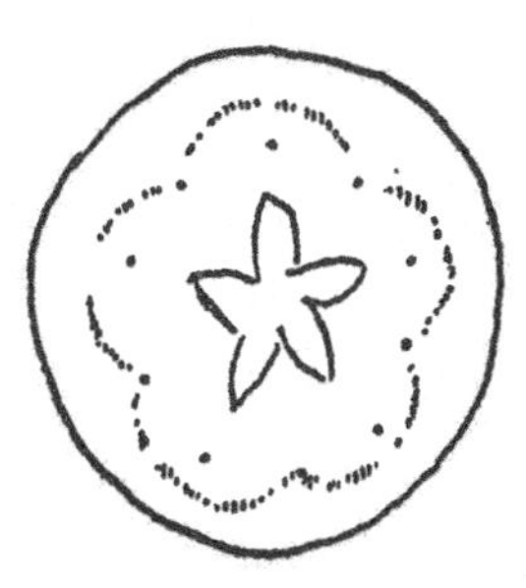

Fig. 5

The star that is seen in the cross-section of an apple (especially the star apple) not only reminds us of the five-pointed star but also of its five-part blossom.

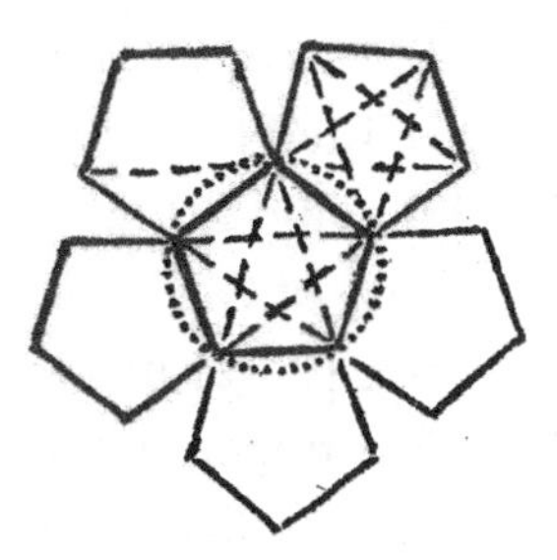

Fig. 6

times, creating a perfect hexagon, which can then be repeated *ad infinitum* (see figure 2). The luminous rock crystal (figure 3) and the cells of the honeycomb are examples. The lily, symbol of purity and innocence, is also made up of six parts.

The opposite of the number six in almost all ways is the number five. Where one can dreamily follow the connection of the six with the circle, a division of a circle in five equal pieces asks for much *knowledge* and *consciousness*. Five is not woven into the cosmos, it stands apart, it is "independent." No wonder the five-pointed pentagram (figure 4) has always been a symbol for "evil." But it can also repel evil (recall Dr. Faust, who fastened a pentagram to his door).

The apple belongs to the family Rosaceae. In cross-section, the apple reveals a natural pentagram, a living five-pointed star (figure 5)! I don't think we need to say any more (see figure 1).

But the number five does not have to stand alone. If we go from a flat surface into three-dimensional space, the five can connect with the twelve in twelve symmetrical planes, the pentagonal dodecahedron whose every plane has five sides (figure 6). In other words, if the five, seen as "distanced" and "bad," is taken out of two dimensions and lifted into three dimensions, it can be reintegrated into the cosmos by connecting with the cosmic totality of twelve (remember the world totality of the twelve constellations of the zodiac). The same is true for the independence of humanity. If humanity is lifted from its "flat" level, in which egotism and thus evil resides, and brought to a higher dimension by absorbing the impulse of Christ, this independence can be used as a new and creative power in the world order. In other words, mankind, with its five-fingered hand that naturally wants to perform egotistical deeds, is called to cleanse the earthly five and bring it back to the cosmic connection of twelve. Only then will it be able to set the earth free from darkness and bring back the light of Godly world order.

Once again we find the main motif of the entire world of fairy tales.

In summary, we have now seen how the old folk tales, which may seem to be nice, friendly, pleasant stories, have a great world history behind them. If we reconsider how a small child can absorb and process, even subconsciously, something so deep, we should remember the enormous divine power that a nursing child is given through breast milk and ask ourselves: "How is it possible that this little being can accept and take in something so great?" The answer can only be understood if we can fathom how these forces work. We then immediately understand that only miraculous breast milk can give a child the foundation for the rest of his life.

## "Sleeping Beauty": a fairy tale about the fall of man and salvation

Let us now look at how one fairy tale expresses the archetype of the path through darkness into new light. In passing, we should stress that our view of the fairy tales should never be seen as a universal explanation. Words can be explained in many different ways and images can be seen from many different angles.

We have chosen the fairy tale "Sleeping Beauty" (Jacob Grimm), the tale of a princess who at the time of her birth receives good gifts from twelve wise fairies and a curse from a thirteenth fairy. We all know the rest of the story.

When a human soul descends into the world and is born on earth, it is accompanied by heavenly powers that give it cosmic strengths and abilities that it will need in its new life. We must look for the home of these heavenly powers in the transcendental worlds of the stars. There are twelve large realms in the firmament of the stars: the twelve constellations of the zodiac that emanate certain divine-cosmic powers. This world of cosmic star-powers, which ancient, clairvoyant mankind was still able to see, grew out of this old consciousness and has thus existed for far longer than the written-down present-day studies of astronomy and astrology. The twelve fairies in the tale can be seen to represent the heavenly powers that gave the soul cosmic gifts from the twelve realms of the zodiac. The destiny of the soul is determined largely through the way these powers enter the soul, which can depend on various factors. In ancient times destiny was thus almost completely determined. Today this is less the case. The soul's character, powers and possibilities also partly come forth from the gifts that the divine powers can bestow upon it. However, the thirteenth fairy, who was not invited and wants revenge, comes before the twelfth. She declares that the girl will prick her finger on the spinning wheel and die on her fourteenth birthday. The twelfth fairy cannot undo this curse but can change death into one hundred years of sleep.

During the development of mankind, the adversary, who was not included in the plan of the creator (that is, he was not "invited" to participate), came to mankind and brought him onto the path that would ultimately lead him to ruin. After this disturbance, Christ came. He was not able to undo the adversary's deed but could give mankind much higher possibilities: the possibility to lift himself from the darkness into the light once again. Christ changed the descent into darkness into a temporary state, "one hundred years of sleep." The "100 years of sleep" imagery used in the fairy tale should be seen as "a very long time." Thus, what the twelfth fairy did in the tale can be seen as a Christian impetus.

The king subsequently orders all spinning wheels in the kingdom to be burned. But destiny cannot be thwarted, and when the princess turns fourteen, something strange happens. She suddenly feels a strong desire to get to know every dark nook and cranny of the castle.

At around fourteen, every physically maturing child starts to show interest in every part of her earthly haven, (her body). She has ardent interest in how the eye is formed, how hearing works, how the skeleton is built.

And then the young princess arrives at the small attic room, which she never knew existed, and sees an old woman at a spinning wheel.

While getting to know all these unknown areas, the fourteen-year-old child also discovers her attic room: her head, in which thoughts are spun. "Spinning thoughts" is grown-up when compared to the playing, singing, and jumping around of small children: we see an "old woman" who sits spinning at the wheel.

However, this old woman is actually the evil thirteenth fairy who tempts the princess into trying the spinning wheel herself, in other words, to thinking independently, or to committing her own "Fall." Her fate is sealed: she pricks her finger and falls into a deep sleep.

This part of the story is similar to the apparent death of Snow White. But why this prick?

Thought, as we see it here, or knowledge, has a sharp character (think of the splinter in Kay's eye). We speak of someone's "keen" or "sharp" intelligence, we even see a pointed nose on the clever fox. Sleeping Beauty pricks her finger on intelligence, and falls asleep.

This should surprise us and make us ask: does this make sense? A child who has discovered and is using logical reasoning for the first time should wake up! But as a result of the awakening to the world of the senses, mankind falls asleep to the world of the soul. When a person wakes up in the morning, she takes leave of the world in which the soul abides during sleep. When a child matures to being able to think independently, the divine world in which she has lived dreamily until now closes. Thus, after the time of Abraham and Moses, who could still meet God, all mankind has "fallen asleep" into modern materialistic thought. We are all in the middle of Sleeping Beauty's "one hundred years of soul sleep."

When Sleeping Beauty dozes off, everything that lives in the castle falls asleep. Not only the human beings, but also the animals, even the fly on the wall and the fire in the hearth. This image shows how all the world is included in the "Fall of Mankind." Mankind and the world can only develop together as one. As soon as humanity isolated itself, the whole world suffered and fell into a pitiful existence. It is easy to imagine how mankind could take the whole world with him in his Fall.

In the Oberufer Paradise Play, we see this portrayed in the descent of utter darkness when Adam bites into the apple.

The hedge of thorns grows over the castle and envelops it quickly and completely, making it invisible. Something similar happens to us too. When we sleep, the powers of growth and restoring forces continue to work on our body and mend what has been exhausted during the day. However, if we sleep too much, we become lethargic. The powers of growth that we have in common with plants increase uncontrollably and eventually seriously hinder the soul's tasks. But rampant growth is also seen in the soul. When our soul (the "I" consciousness) falls asleep, we lose control over our soul life. We become a plaything for our desires and impulses. The "thorns" in our soul grow until we are surrounded by an impenetrable hedge. But let's not forget that this is a hedge of *roses*. The rose has thorns on its stem, but is able to overcome its thorny nature to grow a beautiful flower. This is why the rose is the queen of flowers, not the innocent lily. A reigning queen must be able to control her bad side.

But how can mankind conquer the bad side of a soul that has

developed from selfish and materialistic thought? In other words, how can mankind awaken from this soul sleep?

This is only possible if our true consciousness comes forward and we recognize that we are servants to a higher being. If we realize this, we will feel like *human beings*, personalities, and we will be able to control our impulses. This self-consciousness, the prince in us, takes action.

The prince arrives with sword in hand, forcing the thorny hedges to give way: our self-consciousness is "armed" with a sword that does not inflict wounds (if it remains true to its task) but forces the darkness to give way to light.

Only then will our self-consciousness arise from its soul sleep: the prince kisses Sleeping Beauty and she wakes up.

The wedding that follows is actually a union of our soul with our higher divine principles. These principles lift us out of our small realm into the understanding that we must serve our personal development, and the development of the world.

Sleeping Beauty takes us from the Fall of Mankind to redemption, from our ancient past to the far future of mankind. At the same time, this tale shows us the development of all human life.

Once again, we see how fairy tales engage us in the greater evolution of all mankind through personal development.

## "Mother Holle": the conscious world and the dream world

Let's now look at a fairy tale that works with an especially important image: the difference between the daytime world of wakeful, conscious thinking (the sense world) and the world of our dreams. In other words, the difference between the earth world and the world to which our soul is lifted after death: the spirit world, which is also the origin of every child's soul. This is the tale of "Mother Holle" (Jacob Grimm).

"Once upon a time there was a widow who had two daughters." This first sentence alone speaks volumes. A widow is a woman who has lost her husband: the father of the girls is dead.

For the young child, "the father" stands for "Our Father." Fairy tales give small images for large things. This fairy tale tells us: the World Father is seemingly "dead" for mankind. Many people still believe in God and some still experience Him in some way, but for us His presence is no longer spiritually visible or audible as it was in the time of Abraham. God our Father is just as real as previously but His light shines dimly, as far away as the soul of someone who has passed away.

But who is the mother and who are the daughters?

The young child experiences something of the World Father in the word "father." In much the same way, for the dreaming consciousness of the young child, the mother in fairy tales is experienced as the greatest of known mothers: Mother Earth. This mother gave us our body; she carries us and feeds us and we must work for her. She is our greatest mother. However, she is a "widow." In the beginning, God walked with Adam and Eve in paradise: the World Father lived with Mother Earth. But, after the Fall, the Creator retreated more and more from his creation: Mother Earth became a "widow."

In this fairy tale, the mother has two daughters: one who is sweet and diligent and also quite beautiful (in fairy tales outward appearance also tells us something about inner quality); and one who is unpleasant and lazy also ugly. The mother loves the ugly daughter the most, for she is her real daughter; the beautiful girl is her stepdaughter. This is why the beautiful daughter is forced to work hard and is badly treated. On the other hand, the ugly daughter has a wonderful life of ease.

Here we see an image of how lazy people who don't feel like exerting themselves in their tasks for Mother Earth take from her abundance, while the diligent, hard-working people who strive for positive goals must often live a meager life. Their modesty makes them the "stepchildren" of Widow Earth. A clean, enlightened soul lives within them. The lazy people who live in luxury are completely tied to the "earthly" side of life; they are Mother Earth's "own children." However, their souls can be called "ugly" because of their inferior orientation.

The pretty girl must sit and spin at the wheel all day, until her fingers bleed. In our blood we find our personality, our "I." In Goethe's *Faust*, Dr. Faust signed his pact with the devil with a drop of blood. If people fulfill their earthly tasks with dedication (like the pretty girl), their true selves will come forward: they seal their actions with their blood.

Also, see how the spinning wheel serves a different purpose in this fairy tale than in "Sleeping Beauty." In "Sleeping Beauty" the spinning wheel tempted the princess into doing the forbidden (image of the Fall). In this tale, one can see how the diligent person doesn't turn his back on sober work that just has to be done and in a way "spins" his logical thoughts. The work is done with dedication for the benefit of someone else (the girl spins for her stepmother). Through this Christian impulse, the work that originally stems from the Fall into darkness is also freed.

The girl now goes to the well to wash the blood off her spindle. The diligent person wants to rid her work of spots. But this is not possible. The work continues to be connected to the person who did it. The spindle sinks into the water: the work that was done is absorbed into the element water, i.e. in the life of the earthly world.

After receiving a severe scolding from her mother, the girl jumps into the well to look for the spindle and sinks to the bottom. For a short moment she loses consciousness, but when she awakens, she finds herself in a lush field with beautiful flowers and singing birds. We know that people who are on the brink of drowning experience a glimpse of the spiritual world. In relation to this we can recall John the Baptist, who immersed his followers in the river Jordan. They too temporarily lost consciousness and caught a glimpse of the spiritual world. In a certain way, they were initiated in the Holy Spirit. The girl who sinks into the well and ends up in a lush field can also be seen as an image of the soul that is initiated in the spirit world, or as passing through the gates of death and returning to the spiritual world.

For the girl to reach a "higher" world (that is, "heaven") while *falling* seems absurd. However, depth and height are related in the spiritual sense. By *diving into* the life of the soul, one can reach great *heights* in the spiritual sense. Later in in the tale, it becomes evident that one should actually think of a "higher" level in the fairy tale. When the girl fluffs Mother Holle's duvet she makes it "snow" on earth!

The succulent meadow, full of flowers, in which the child finds herself, is an image for the threshold of the spiritual world, brimming with life. Here the soul meets hitherto unknown growth forces. While walking through this meadow, the girl passes an oven. The rolls in the oven call to her, saying: "Take us out of the oven. We are more than done!" During the Last Supper, Christ called his body bread—nourishment that is created by human hands joining sun and earth. At this moment, the young girl meets that which is blessed by Christ and she knows how to accept and treat it. A bit further on, she walks under an apple tree and the apples call to her, saying: "Little girl, shake us out of this tree! We are all very ripe!" Here she meets nature, created by the Divine, and she once again knows how to handle these gifts and carefully collects the apples.

Once she has received the gifts from both the Father and the Son, she sees a house. An ugly old woman is sitting in the window. She is so ugly that the young girl wants to run away at first. But the woman speaks to her in a friendly manner and invites her in.

Anyone who follows spiritual training must endure various tests. This is necessary because a higher development carries higher responsibilities. The tests that must be endured create the needed maturity. Someone who is on the verge of entering the spiritual world will have to endure even more rigorous tests. Spiritual science has described how the developing soul meets a monstrous, frightening being, the so-called Guardian, who prevents unready human souls from entering the higher worlds. The girl, walking through the "threshold to the spiritual world," must endure these tests. The ugly woman is the Guardian. But the good child is allowed to pass through; her soul is found to be ready and, after the old woman has beckoned her, she hesitantly enters the old woman's home: the spiritual world.

The girl's new mistress, "Mother Holle," now gives the girl instructions as to what she must do. The most important task is fluffing the old woman's bed every day. This must be done so vigorously that the down feathers fly about in the room. The girl performs her task so diligently that the people on earth continuously cry: "It's snowing again today!"

Souls that live in the spiritual world can bestow something of their spiritual benefits onto the people on earth. On All Soul's Day, we remember the dead, but few people suspect how much the dead *help* us throughout the year in our daily lives if we are able to open our hearts to them. Divine gifts, for example in the way of a sudden bright idea, are given silently and unnoticed much like "soft, white snowflakes" that fall lightly on our heads. How beautiful is the image of the girl who lets "snow" fall from the spiritual to the earthly world! At the same time, snow signifies complete and utter purity coming from the heavens onto earth so that the earth can be released from darkness.

After having faithfully served Mother Holle for some time, the girl begins to long for her mother, even though she had always been very hard on her.

Mother Holle praises her highly for her longing. With this longing, the girl shows she has not forgotten her difficult task on earth.

This "homesickness" for her life on earth is a prelude to the end of the fairy tale, in which the girl returns to her strict mother, in other words to Mother Earth. This part of the fairy tale describes an important, fundamental part of our development: the human soul's cyclical return to earth from the spiritual world. In much the same way, the soul returns to conscious life on earth, where activities and development are resumed after having spent the night in the dream world. In the greater scope of things, the soul also returns to the work world, the earthly world, after a much longer time in the spiritual world (between death and rebirth) in order to continue with challenges that were left unfinished in the last life and to develop in an ever more spiritual sense. This is the ancient and well-known principle of rebirth or reincarnation, which was confirmed as completely true by theosophy and anthroposophy.

For the soul, returning to earth is a serious task. Earth is the world of both physical and spiritual labor and therefore the world of tests that must be endured to ensure continuing development. Each time, the soul must return to earth and begin a new life, while returning to the spiritual world is actually a liberation. This is perhaps why babies enter the earthly world crying, and those who pass on often have a smile on their faces. It is burdensome for the soul to enter the earthly world, and a blessing to be able to return to the Fatherland, the spiritual world.

However, the human soul that lives in the spiritual world feels and cannot ignore that the tasks and tests needed for further development await it in the earthly world. Thus, after having remained in the spiritual world for a certain amount of time and being filled with enormous willpower to develop further, it longs to return to its work world—Earth.

Mother Holle allows the girl to return. But first she will receive what she has earned. Mother Holle brings her to a gate—we could call it the "gate of reincarnation"—that brings her back to the earthly world. Here Mother Holle returns the spindle to her. She can now continue to work on spinning the thread of life's experiences and achievements. The everlasting development of the human soul is depicted in this image. Gold rains upon her. As we saw in "Sleeping Beauty," when the soul prepares itself for a new life on earth, powers from all parts of the cosmos flow to her: new life powers. The type and amount of powers that come depend, among others, on the nature of the development of the soul. A highly developed soul attracts many richly varied cosmic powers for new life, while a soul with limited development only attracts a few. This cosmic "gift" with which the soul enters earthly life continues to work throughout this life. In "Mother Holle" it is depicted by a rain of gold instead of the gifts that Sleeping Beauty received from the fairies. The gold that rains on the girl does not leave her—it gives her an indelible glow for the rest of her life. She now passes the gate into the earthly world. The rooster crows to the new day. She enters her new life glowing.

We can now briefly discuss the other, lazy girl. She is her sister's opposite in every way. She does not accept the gifts of the Son nor of the Father and does not let it "snow" on earth. While standing at the gate to her new life, golden rain does not wash over her, but instead black tar: the insignificantly developed soul receives a scarce amount of qualities and new life powers, as said above, allowing the darker sides to come forward. These also remain with her for the rest of this earthly life.

And here the fairy tale ends. Those who listen to it experience how goodness, if not on earth then in the spiritual world, is rewarded and evil is "punished" with unfavorable consequences. It also shows how new possibilities are opened to goodness while they are crushed by evil. Thus, the discrepancy between good and evil and the consequences for both, even through the gates of death and new life, play an important role in this fairy tale.

If one does not want to end this fairy tale with the dark side of good and evil, then a personal ending can be created. Rudolf Steiner pointed out how important it is that fairy tales give a joyful and positive impulse to children by ending on a positive note (see "What about happy endings," below). To end "Mother Holle" on a positive note, we could say, " . . .but the shining girl did not forget her dark sister, who had been chased away by her mother. She went into the wide world to look for her so that she could chase her darkness away with her brilliant gold. Who knows, maybe she will find her one day!" As for us adults, we can remember that this is the task of everyone who is able to spiritually shine on earth.

---

**ENDNOTES**

1 See, for example, Hélène Jacquet, *Christmas Plays from Oberufer* (Great Barrington, MA: SteinerBooks 2007).

2 See also "Schuld en Onschuld"("Guilt and Innocence") in Daniel Udo de Haes, *Zonnegeheimen* (Sun Secrets) (Zeist, Netherlands: Vrij Geestesleven, 1951-1986).

# 2 | The world of the young child

## How do young children experience their surroundings?

Now that we have gotten to know the world of fairy tales, let us look at the young child. The thoughts and feelings that exist in young children and the way they go through deep experiences is so far removed from our consciousness and soul life that we can only try to feel our way into understanding. And it is important not to ignore it. Today there is hardly any other phase in life that needs our attention, protection and understanding as much as early childhood.

In order to take the first step, try to remember your own time as a small child. Not specific events; try to return to that time in your life and remember what you *experienced.*

If we practice this and discuss our experiences with others, we will discover that we were fascinated by things that we find completely unremarkable now. Practice will also allow us to observe how the children in our lives show the same fascination for things that we hardly notice. During one of my courses, participants remembered a black dress, the laugh of an old lady, silver knobs on a tea table, and much more. But we can also imagine that there are much simpler things that fascinate a children. Not long ago, I saw two very young ones crouched at the side of the road over a manhole cover. The grooves in the cover were filled with dirt that they were busy extracting with small sticks. They were so entranced by this that nothing else in the world existed for them at that moment. In a way, they had become *one* with that small bit of dirt they were working on. At this moment, in a seemingly futile but actually extremely intensive way, they experienced something of the materialism of the earthly world, an experience completely new for the little child, a quiet intensification of the earth element, not from without but from within. By observing such incidents, listening to what the child is being allowed to experience, and showing the same devotion to these experiences, we hope to concentrate on the essence of the child and may come a little closer to our goal.

Another example of this kind of event took place in the front garden of an orphanage. It was winter, and the thawing snow had formed a large puddle in the middle of the lawn. This unexpected, naturally formed "lake" gave us a wonderful opportunity to observe how intensely little children are connected with their surroundings and how differently they stand in life than adults. The adults who walked past thought the puddle very strange but walked on. What else could they have done? If one of them, just for fun, had put a boat in the puddle or had walked straight through it, the others would have cast him strange glances! But this was totally different for the children! They walked through the water in their rubber boots, played with rafts, and made bridges and dams for hours on end. There was not only the "joy" but also something else. Much like the above incident when the element earth was intensely experienced, this incident allowed the children to give both body and soul to the *element water*. The essence of water, and everything that goes with it, fascinated them. Even more wonderful is the fact that this "big lake" had emerged in a place where there is normally a lawn, or earth. Thus, we can understand how intensely the children experienced the relationship between earth and water while playing in the puddle. They may even (subconsciously) have come closer to the origins of these two elements than we ever will when reading the story of the Creation. Keeping such an experience away from the children would have been a serious infringement on their inner development.

This wonderful water spectacle did not pass without accidents. Some of the children became so intensely connected with this wet element that they entered the house completely soaked. At least there were no detrimental effects. The "casualties" had a wonderful afternoon and were richer for it.

Thus, we must slowly learn to differentiate between what we should forbid the children and what we really cannot keep them from, even if it means dealing with dirty hands, soaked clothes or other discomforts. We must learn to discern what is more important: a quick, undisturbed course of events or the inner development of the child. For someone who works with children on a daily basis it can be difficult to give the latter priority, especially if our work has certain limits. However, if we focus on these things and know what is at stake, we can usually manage quite well and achieve results that are that much more important.

Of course, we don't have to accept *everything* the children do. Sometimes "no" is unavoidable. The important thing is that "no" be given with understanding and empathy and not brusquely, only to avoid adult inconvenience. I once saw a cartoon in an American magazine in which a mother asked her maid: "Oh Mary, can you see what the kids are up to and tell them that whatever they're doing is against the rules?" This may seem exaggerated but is often what happens. Being allowed to play in puddles is of utmost importance for children!

Our technology-obsessed world is an exciting but also a degenerate place for children, making events like playing in puddles that much more important. The element of water heals the children and returns some of the inner life and peace to them that they lose more and more through the effects of modern technology. Don't think that a bath, in which the children can play to their hearts content, is enough. This water is only partly real. In the same way as a lion in a cage is not a completely *real* lion, water from the faucet in a bathtub is not completely *real water* in the full sense! Raindrops, or snow that melts and makes puddles in places where one can normally walk without getting wet feet—*that* is what we call water! Our modern culture that has so many atrocities can be given merits for having produced children's rubber boots! This heals some of the wounds that today's world has brought to the souls of children with its "technical" wonders.

Another interesting fact: we have seen more and more aquariums being placed in neurology wards, especially in the children's ward because they have proven to help with the healing process. A magazine attributed this to the "distraction" of watching the fish swim. But, without a doubt, it is devoting attention to fish, which are completely saturated and one with the *element* "water," that works as medication for these strained souls.

Please don't take what was said above about water from the faucet in a dogmatic way! Playing in the bathtub, although not ideal, can also have a healing effect on children. In the same way, it can be wonderful for a child to be given a small tub of water in which to play or put boats. When done, the peaceful and healthy effect on the child will certainly be noticeable.

The element of fire is much more difficult for children, as technology has not come up with an equivalent to "rubber boots" or "healing aquariums" when it comes to fire. On the contrary, modern technology has created central heating, which has alienated children from this indispensable element. It is no wonder that boys, as soon as they are a bit older, like to play with fire, preferably in a self-made hut or in the forest. Of course, this should not be allowed, as it is dangerous. But if we think of it from the point of view that a child must get to know the element of fire (so difficult in today's world), we will look at and react to "playing with fire" differently and possibly even allow it now that we know the deeper meaning! We may even be able to let the child discover this element in controlled surroundings, for example by letting him burn some old junk in the backyard.

The other elements ("elements" in this context being earth, water, air and fire) must also be discovered, however inconvenient this may be for the parents. The element of air is discovered in whistles, horns, paper windmills, paper airplanes, etc. This can be extremely irritating for us adults, but the children don't seem to tire of getting to know how air behaves, all its characteristics.

Another game that will engage children with the element of air and which is less stressful for adults is flying a kite. What a wonderful and inspiring way to lift the imagination to a higher level, to the powerful airstreams that circle the earth way up high!

Children meet the element of earth most actively while digging. We have already seen a small example of this above. Once again, adults can be confronted with certain complications when their children come inside covered in dirt after having dug a cave. Children are oblivious to the fact that they are covered in dirt and will only realize it when they are scolded. For the development of the child it is of utmost importance that the adult not only accepts the dirty clothes but also empathizes with the wonderful encounter this child has had with Mother Earth and the deep bond that can now be developed.

Not only for practical but also for moral reasons, forbidding certain activities may be needed and can also work positively. For example, we should certainly forbid cursing, ridiculing, disrespect, wanting to break something. It can give a child backbone and help him in his development if these actions are forbidden in a loving, empathizing way.

Rudolf Steiner asks us to be careful when we forbid children under three years old to do certain things. What does he mean? When a little child reaches to grab a beautiful vase, for example, this is done because he has come to earth to get to know the earthly world through his *senses*. This is a holy task for the child, and it permeates his entire being. If the adult now says: "Don't touch!" then the (subconscious) reaction is: "My parents forbid something that God has bade me to do." The shock that this brings to the soul life of this child hardly needs mentioning. However, the vase need not be broken. A tactful solution is to take the vase in one's own hands and let the child touch and look at it. Then the child's longing is satisfied and the vase stays in one piece.

## Children who reject fairy tales

We live in a time in which children mature early. Parents are more inclined to material things and have (partly) lost the natural ability to lead their children during their lives. Many parents see their children as their peers at a very early age and let them decide for themselves what they do or do not want. We even see this happening with young children. For example, if a child does not like fairy tales, they are not "imposed" on him and thus he may be deprived of them throughout his life.

It is true that imposing a fairy tale on a child does not make sense. This would accomplish the opposite of the intended goal. However, we must not forget that what fairy tales tell us has great importance not only for some but for *all* children. One should try to understand how the truly good fairy tales give every human child the chance to become part of the greater creation and the entire development of mankind, as discussed earlier. This is the larger task given to everyone who comes to the earthly world. We will then see that fairy tales are an essential part of a child's development. The most important thing is to tell the tales in a way that reaches all children.

Let's imagine a child fascinated by technology, interested only in cars and wall sockets. Her interest has been triggered not only by her natural ability but also through modern technology, with its traffic, radios, and televisions and people who try to make themselves heard above the noise. This child is not interested in stories fit for her age group. She criticizes the most beautiful fairy tales saying: "That can't be true. A frog can't change into a human being!" End of story.

We can compare these children, who have become victims of the modern world, to plants who have had too little water: they have dried up. If we water them, the dried roots will not absorb the water immediately. Should we then decide to not give any more water? The plant will certainly die. We should try and find the right rhythm of dosage and give the nourishment with love and devotion in order for the plant to eventually be able to absorb the water and return to life. We can often only make contact with these children through those things that interest them: model cars, Disney pictures, etc. This is where we should start, slowly working our way to the actual fairy tales and games and the truly beautiful pictures that appeal to the ever-healthier imagination (see "The craving for 'new' and 'true' stories," below).

## Clutter

An important point when dealing with young children is the clutter that they leave behind and the question of whether to teach them to clean up after themselves. This may be very desirable from the point of view of the parent who is at home with the child. Once again, it depends on what motivates the adult: an understanding of what lives in the child and what is needed for his development, or a dislike of clutter in the house.

What happens if we expect a small child to clean up *on his own*? This question is more important for the child than we may think. It goes without saying that we can't let even the youngest child play endlessly. His play must be stopped for meals and bedtime. We can then also want him to put his toys away, as long as we do this with empathy and don't speak of the toys as "clutter." For example, we can ask the child to put the doll to bed or say that the horse should really head to its stable so that it can also go to sleep. Young children are sanguine by nature; changes are made quickly and are easily endured. The child will continue his play peacefully after the meal or the following day.

However, if we use an angry tone to tell the child that he has made a mess and that this can't happen again, we actually say something completely different. We want or even expect him to clean up after himself. We can only understand what this means for the child if we realize that during play he is in a fantasy world, a dream world. If we expect him to wake up out of this dream world on his own, we are actually demanding something like: tonight, I want you to wake up at midnight all on your own.

If a child is captivated by a certain toy, he will only lay it aside if his fantasy has ended or he becomes enticed by another toy. If we ask him to say to himself: "Fine, but I first have to clean up the other toy," we actually ask him to consciously awaken out of his fantasy world into our business-like "reality." This is impossible for him and if we demand it, it will have a deadening effect on his imagination. If we were to do so, we would contribute to a premature awakening of plain knowledge, detrimental to the development of organs as well as the brain. This will cause the child to stay behind physically, emotionally, and in his possibility for extensive thinking: something that we see daily in the modern child!

One of the most important games for every healthy child is making a "house" or "hut" and living in it. Together with a brother, sister, or friend, tablecloths are pulled half off the table, sheets and blankets are taken off newly made beds, and any other piece of material is used to cover areas that are still open. Heavy objects such as teapots, wine carafes, a stack of plates, etc. (the children are oblivious to the fact that these objects might be valuable or breakable) are placed on top of the table to keep everything from slipping down. Now it's time to furnish the home. A box becomes a closet, the waste paper basket becomes the stove, a couple of chairs on their sides create a new room, and the children, while "building," "live" in their newly created home. Once they have finished building, the game is usually finished, but while playing they feel completely at home in this cozy place, a feeling that will not be repeated at any other time during the rest of their lives.

What do they experience during this play?

Every human soul that comes to earth from the spiritual world is given a home: her very own, small body. The soul has helped build this home during pregnancy and continues to build it after birth, assisted by spiritual powers. The soul is imbued with this divine task: building her "home" on earth and feeling "at home" in it. This task is so important that she cannot help but continue her divine task outside the body as well. In much the same way, ancient civilizations had "symbolic" actions to accompany certain religious ceremonies. Building a "home" is a deeply religious act for children. However, we must remember that religion and devotion mean profound joy and happiness for the child and that every childish joy should actually be seen as deep devotion.

How should we react to this building of "homes" by children?

Let's imagine the following: a mother is on her way home from work and plans to quickly set the table when she comes home. She enters the house and sees chaos! She scolds the children who have created this chaos: "What *have* you done! Look at this mess! And now I'll have to . . ." etc. This is understandable but does not soften the impact of the scolding. Think of it in this way. What if Moses, who received divine inspiration to build the Tabernacle, was told by another angry god that he had done something bad? For the small child, a parent who gives such an angry scolding can be compared to such an angry god. One can imagine what a conflict such an event will create in the child's soul, which is only focused on its divine task. It is of the utmost importance that we as parents learn to control ourselves and, instead of scolding, place ourselves in the world of the children and empathize with them. We must learn to do this without a show or uttering complimentary ooh's and aah's, but from within. We should try to find a way to be genuinely happy for the child, to find the deeper significance of his actions even if this means setting the table with the hut still in place underneath.

In the part about spring in my series *Zonnegeheimen*[1] I tried to describe something about the spiritual background of searching for a home on earth for children older than 7 through the parable: "How man found his dwelling on earth."[2]

It should now also be clear that the topic of "cleaning up" applies to school-age children, and not the younger ones.

## The young child and crafts

The relationship between adults and small children is clearly visible in *crafts*. In olden times, every craft was seen as a kind of mystery, as a type of calling. Young children still experience this calling, although unconsciously. When a small boy plays "bus driver," he still experiences the wonder of something that was only possible for the spirit: moving over the earth without the use of one's legs. He also feels pride because he can distribute profound things to people: the pieces of paper with those mysterious symbols on them are full of concealed secrets for the small child. A "real" bus driver "learned" his trade and has lost all contact with the mysteries of his craft.

When a young child enters a carpenter's workshop (assuming these still exist), she will be fascinated by the smell of bare wood, the flame-like design of the grain, the workman's tools and how they are used. The perfectly round curls that emerge from the wood plane show her living geometry. The carpenter smiles. He "knows" that this is all "normal." It belongs, consciously or not, to the honors of the trade to disregard these things because it demonstrates how often he has already experienced them. Imagine a carpenter who becomes elated every time a curl is formed. He would be seen as a beginner and therefore not as an experienced carpenter. This is why he smiles—but in this smile he is not conscious of the fact that the young child still has a "dreaming" and therefore very real connection with the deeper essence of his craft, from which his own soul has been closed off.

We adults must look at these early childhood experiences in full consciousness and with understanding interest. Only then can we protect the children from disenchantment and discreetly lead them to something good.[3]

## Ordinary things

In the beginning of this chapter we asked why small children can be so completely fascinated by what we consider mundane things. We dove deeper into some specific situations. Now we would like to try and look more generally, leading us directly to fairy tales.

We might say that "small children see many things for the first, or almost the first, time, which is why they find them so special." But if we look more closely we will see that this is incorrect. Let's look at it in the following way.

If we are spoken to in a certain language, we will only be able to know what is being said if we understand that language. In other words, we will only be able to understand if that language is already "alive within us."

In a similar way, someone who sees a mountain for the first time, for example, can only be deeply impressed by it if he carries something of the essence of a "mountain," of the essence of "something uplifted," in his soul. The mountain speaks to the human soul in a "mountain language," the language of the "uplifted." If the human soul carried nothing of the mountain essence within it, there would be no bottom on which the mountain language could land. The language would not be understood and the mountain would mean absolutely nothing.

More generally speaking, if awe is inspired by something, or a connection with something is consciously experienced, it is actually nothing more than a deep "recognition" of this thing that is concealed somewhere in the soul and is abruptly or slowly being awakened by the experience.

This is true for adults as well as children. The question is: Where does this concealed, sleeping connection with things come from? When answering this question, we will see how differently the explanation manifests itself in adults and children.

Let's first look at an example from the world of the adult.

In the Byzantine school of painting, the Italian primitives (such as Cimabue) and especially in Russian icons, one sees "the Madonna," "the annunciation," and other religious images painted against a gold background. Why did these early painters surround their figures with gold? Surely this was not only because of tradition or some specific religious feeling and even less through intellectual reflection! There was a much deeper need that drove them. They could not have painted it differently. But why not?

Before birth, while still in the holy "Father-land," these people had absorbed the impulse of Christianity in their souls. They arrived on earth completely saturated by this pre-birth Christianity. They actually already carried Christian history and traditions deeply hidden within their souls and subconsciously recognized them when they encountered them in earthly life. Thus, every such experience was a "divine recognition," not conscious, but deeply unconscious or half-conscious. When painting a Madonna, these painters felt that the paintings could only be complete if they surrounded the Virgin Mother with the golden glow of her, and their, truly existing "spiritual Fatherland."

The recognition of the soul in young children has similar origins. In adults we recognize the soul in nature, art, religion, philosophy—in short, in culture. In young children we find it in the most everyday things—a chair, a table, a spoon, a flower, a bird—as well as in the strong connection of the child's relationship to the "elements": earth, water, air, fire as previously described. Please don't think that young children's "recognitions of the soul" in "regular objects" are less important than those of adults. The opposite is true! Because the divine world from before birth is still so much closer to these small children and enables them to connect so intensely with the essence of things, the small child lives much more deeply in the soul world than do adults. As we saw in his encounter with crafts, the young child's soul experience is more primitive and therefore much deeper and broader than ours. We stand in the stream of culture with our soul connection while the child, who has a profound connection with "everyday things," stands closer to the origins of creation.

The awe a small child feels when encountering new things in his surroundings is awe for the new, the unknown. However, the complete submission to the things he observes comes from a dreamy remembrance of what is carried deep within and comes from the pre-birth world.

Many of us who can accept the inner connection of the young child to plants, animals, sounds, and colors may still be surprised when we hear of her pre-birth connection to ordinary things such as baskets, a spoon, or a cupboard. But the essence of these things, not their tangible form, also has its origins in the spiritual world. They are likewise spiritual principles that have been brought to their earthly form by mankind. It is the development, this "birth process" of spiritual origin to earthly form through human hands, that the small child perceives with her whole being and for which she has deep inner respect.

Let's take a table, for example. A table is tangible, born of human hands. But this human creation represents sacrifice and unselfishness. The archetypal table is an altar. In the spiritual world, there are also altars to which angels bring offerings to higher angel beings.

The chair represents hospitality and mildness. It invites us to come and sit and rest for a while. In heaven there are also many chairs, with one being the highest of them all: God the Father's throne. This throne and these chairs are the archetype of a king's throne but also of the chair in our sitting room. A door is the passage to another room, a gateway, and in the spiritual world it is a passage to a higher level. At the end of our lives, we pass through the gateway of death. The principle of a cabinet that holds our valuables can be found in our hearts, which can harbor the most beautiful secrets. The entire spiritual world is an immense shrine containing wonders that we will only be able to attain if we can find the key. The hammer, with its straight, proud, strong-in-"I"-power shape, is seen in mythology as the divine, well-aimed hammer of Donar and Thor. We could go on and on.

When observing all these "similarities" that the sense world gives us, we must remember that the objects we can see with our eyes—a hammer, a cabinet, a door, a chair or table—are transient. They will no longer be there after a few years or centuries. However, the spiritual principles—Thor's hammer, the divine shrine, the gateway to heaven, God's throne, and the heavenly altars—are eternal. Goethe said, "Alles Vergängliche ist nur ein Gleichnis" (everything we see around us, everything that is transient, is a likeness of its eternal spiritual principle). Young children continually, dreamingly experience this. If we can identify with this dreamy experience, we will be able to come closer to and connect with the essence of the young child.

It should be self-evident that a baby lives in a much stronger connection with his pre-birth origins than does a young child. Because his experiences are much less conscious, "recognition" has a deeper, more dreamy character. He lives almost entirely *in* his divine origins. At kindergarten age, when the senses start to play a more important role, a child experiences two contrasting worlds: the spiritual world and the sense world. Seeing these two worlds meet is what fascinates the child. He dreamily recognizes everything he sees and hears, as if he is the earthly embodiment of something from the spiritual world that still lives within him.[4]

Everything changes after the kindergarten years. Whereas a baby does *not yet* experience the "fascination" of a kindergartner, the school-age child experiences little or no fascination with "everyday" objects. In the adolescent this type of experience is almost entirely gone—the connection with the spiritual origins of objects has almost completely disappeared. The "fascination" with the *meeting of the two worlds* is unique to young children, and can only be rediscovered by adults through conscious practice and deep thought on the essence of things.

The following example illustrates how a child is bound to the essence of objects.

Near my home there is a field where a good amount of junk was dumped years ago: dented pots and pans, leaky kettles, damaged shoes, old mattresses. One day, my youngest daughter, about four years old at the time, came skipping from the field holding up an object. "Look Daddy!" she cried, "Can I hang this up in the living room?" What she had in her hand was an old enameled sign advertising cigarettes. The larger-than-life pack of cigarettes was precisely depicted on a background of bright yellow and red. Naturally, the sign hung in our living room for some time afterwards. I am quite sure that Rembrandt's *The Night Watch* would not have been as interesting to my daughter. The precise illustration of the *object*, the packet, and especially the bright red and yellow fascinated her. She experienced something of their origins in these pure colors.

In this case, teaching the child that a sign advertising cigarettes is "ugly" and "worthless" and does not belong in the living room would have meant that we adults, who are in charge here on earth, could not value the essence of the child, something with which he is completely imbued. What would become of us?

Not only does the young child *recognize* the essence of the object as a whole but also every small part, every knob, leaf, and flower; not only the head of a horse but also the nostrils and hooves; the beak of a bird, a wing, a leg, a talon. Everything reminds him and awakens part of the divine principle within him. Sounds, tones, colors—as we spoke about shortly above—yes, even the world of forms—the roundness of an opening, the four corners of a box—express their essence in a deep language.

We can now understand, through this deep connection with the simplest things, why the old fairy tales speak with such love of these objects. These mundane things often have something special to say: the spindle of the spinning wheel, Cinderella's shoe, Tom Thumb's pebbles and bread crumbs, Snow White's apple, the wishing-table, the cudgel in the sack, and so on.

But we also have a golden crown, a golden throne, a king's castle. Looking at people, we have swineherds and gooseherds, stable boys, princes, princesses, kings, queens, all the normal and abnormal things and people, and finally animals that speak in their own wonderful language of images.

Fairy tales rarely speak of higher worlds or higher spiritual beings. Angels and heaven are hardly ever mentioned. Instead, we meet fairies and gnomes, dragons and witches, whom we see as images of both good and evil spiritual powers. For the child, these beings represent the many forms of good and evil that exist *on earth*.

So why is it that fairy tales don't speak of these higher worlds and spiritual beings when they bear witness to the spiritual world?

To answer this question we must remember that fairy tales were written in a time when humanity still had to find a stronger connection with the *earthly world*, just as the early childhood classroom must. If these tales had told early people (after the mythological period!) about angels and higher beings, they would have held people back instead of helping them to find their way to earth. Fairy tales want to show humanity the right way on the path of the development of mankind, in the same way as they want to show young children which way they should go: *from heaven to earth*.

Each human being must enter the earthly world accompanied by the complete soul content that he brought with him from the pre-birth world. And in this way the small child must also enter the earthly world and look for the "simplest" things. Only then can humanity eventually *consciously* rediscover the spiritual world in its *earthly personification*. Only when humanity *dreamily* recognizes the spiritual world on earth in early childhood can full consciousness for what has been born from the soul into the earthly world awaken.

However, this consciousness must arise at the right time, and not too early. This is why mundane (and also extraordinary) earthly things carry their spiritual content in a lively but deeply concealed way in fairy tales. Much like the germ cell that is protected from premature sprouting by the seed's hard shell, the earthly image in fairy tales is protected from premature discovery, only to reveal its secret later in life, when the soul is in its spring and ripe for the epiphany.

Fairy tales endow the child with an unparalleled, concealed treasure of spiritual germ cells so that the soul can bear the spiritual blossoms when the time is ripe.

Thus, we have a new answer to the question posed at the beginning of this book: "Why do we tell fairy tales to children?"

---

**ENDNOTES**

1 See Daniel Udo de Haes, *Zonnegeheimen* (*Sun Secrets*) (Zeist, Netherlands: Vrij Geestesleven, 1951-1986).

2 Ibid.

3 See, e.g., Daniel Udo de Haes, *The Singing, Playing Kindergarten* (WECAN 2015).

4 Electric toys, toys with motors, and toys that turn or walk powered by a mechanism, are exceptions. The interest that today's kindergartners have for these toys does not come from the pre-birth world. These interests, especially in very young children, must be replaced by arousing their interest in healthier forms. For more on this subject, see Herbert Hahn, *Vom Ernst des Spielens: eine zeitgemässe Betrachtung über Spielzeug und Spiel* (Germany, Waldorfschul-Spielzeug & Verlag, 1930.

# 3 | A few more thoughts on early childhood and fairy tales

## Why metaphors and not concepts?

In our modern time, which values intellect and intellectual understanding above all else, people may ask: Why can't we give the young child more logical concepts that are so much closer to us as adults, along with the extensive and important metaphors of fairy tales?

The most obvious answer is that young children are not yet open for logic. Children who are logical regrettably sacrifice their imaginations and the powers they need to build their organs. It is good if a small child cannot understand sharply defined concepts. Being ahead in development is actually detrimental to the development of a child.

Understanding is static. It cannot grow or change, and is therefore completely unsuitable for the child who is in a dynamic stage of development. Rudolf Steiner says that giving a child a concept to carry for the rest of her life is like giving her a pair of shoes she must wear for the rest of her life.

An image that does not have strict boundaries and therefore remains alive can grow freely with the soul of the child and change to suit the child's development.

The growth process usually happens in a disguised way. Let me explain. When I was learning to be a curative educator I sometimes had to deal with extremely difficult, big boys. Sometimes this was so hard that I thought I would not be able to go on. I became desperate. But just when I had a mind to give up, a thought came up which I did not know was still alive in me: an image from a fairy tale. I suddenly saw a young girl in my mind's eye, a poor girl who had been given the task to spin straw into golden threads. This was impossible for her and she began to cry until suddenly a gnome stood before her who had come to help her accomplish this impossible task. This imagination gave me such confidence that I could pluck up the courage to continue with my difficult task.

I do not want to suggest too much with this story. The powers that helped me and gave me new courage would have had little to do with gnomes. But we don't have to go into detail. The message is: If I had not heard this fairy tale in my early youth, this image would never have surfaced. I would probably have even rejected it if someone had mentioned it to me at that critical moment. However, the truth is that this image was dormant in me for almost thirty years, without me knowing it. I must have heard this tale when I was about four years old. I don't remember. When the image surfaced, I knew exactly what it meant and that it must have been given to me years ago. I felt how powerful it had become after twenty-eight years of concealment. It was not the image itself but the power that it had developed in me in silence through all those years that gave me the courage and strength to go on.

Another possibility is that the images evolve as we grow and as such are completely lost, but at the same time are like sourdough and continue to be present throughout our lives. Their influence is imperceptible, much as the sun's rays cannot be found in the earth but their influence makes seeds sprout. These images work in much the same way on the soul—their work is indiscernible and secretive yet gives the child physical and soul powers. Thus, we find a new answer to the question: how can giving young children images that have such incredible content, sometimes unfathomable to us adults, be good?

First of all, it should be evident from our previous discussions that early childhood's inner essence, so much closer to the divine origins of these images, stands infinitely more open to the content than we do, even though we can *understand* more of it with our intellect! Secondly, *everyone* should be able to feel that it is the images with the greatest content that work most deeply on the development of the child, even when the images are "lost" in the subconscious and never surface.

## The cabbage and the stork

A subject that forces us to speak to children with imagery is birth. Today there is a tendency to disclose all truths to children from early on. There is nothing wrong with the truth, so why should we keep them from children?

Those who think like this overlook that a process such as birth, something we adults do not see as ugly, is made up of many links that stem from the Fall of Adam and Eve. Those of us who know the Oberufer Paradise Play will remember that when the angel banned Adam and Eve from paradise, he bade them labor for their daily bread and suffer pain in bearing children.

Spiritual science teaches us that humanity has been condensed into the physical body more and more since the Fall. The physical body was much less solid before the Fall, even non-existent in the earliest times. Condensing first started after humanity turned away from God until the body gradually took on its present form. Man was now a full citizen of earth with consequences in all areas. Humanity first led a carefree existence on earth, guided by God. Now he had to toil on earth and take care of his own food, a task that fell on the shoulders of men who needed to bond most intensely with the terrestrial. Today, this is still a man's task. He is farmer, clockmaker, artist, or office worker, and must always "work *his* field" (that is, work on his earthliness); through toil and sweat he must earn food for himself and his family. For the woman, the emphasis is on bearing and raising the offspring, of which the former, now that humanity has been condensed into the physical body, will be painful.

Similarly, the young child must find his way to earth. Seeing and experiencing the work traditionally done by the man, the "crafts," can help him. Every craft shows how man can condense something of the divine world into earthly material. This is especially visible in the work of an artist, but can also be seen in other crafts. The traditionally female crafts—housekeeper, seamstress—are no exceptions. Everything done by human hands shows the child how humanity can allow the spirit to enter the earthly world.

Physical birth, however, is something completely different. What happens here does not show how humanity allows the spirit to live on earth through his achievements. The bearer herself does not create. The mother is subjected to the experience with painful contractions. What happens physically during birth has little to do with what happens spiritually. However, the kindergartner still lives primarily in the spiritual world and his dreamy constitution is not yet ready for the physicality of birth. So it is pointless, even harmful, to tell young children about the physical birth process, as this can disrupt their connection to the spiritual side. It should go without saying that prematurely dragging a soul from its spiritual connection has negative consequences for the development of the child!

No wonder that humanity has instinctively created *images* to tell brothers or sisters about a coming birth. Remarkably, these images describe the spiritual birth as the formation of a new body (not to be confused with the physical birth!).

Let's try to imagine what happens here. Led by his guardian angel the human soul comes down from the spiritual world and inhabits the little body that nature has given it. This is where heaven and earth meet: the saying "little children grow from heads of cabbage" says that physical growth springs from the earth. We sometimes even call children "sprouts" or say they "grow like weeds." On the other hand, we say that children are brought by the stork. What a wonderful, angelic image for this great event! The "cabbage" and the "stork" are two images that each show a different side of birth, together creating the whole. In their essence, they are true "fairy tale images" and they can impress upon us the strength of how these images bring great truths, each in their own way. Perhaps this is the seed of a fairy tale that never germinated. For the young child, the image of the stork will be the strongest by far. Only the most phlegmatic child will be able to place the image that the cabbage brings (see "Fairy tales and the temperaments" and "How do we tell different fairy tales for specific temperaments?").

Today, there are probably many people who don't have a connection with imagery who will say that children are brought by angels. Of course, this is also possible. However, this is not an image but the truth, a spiritual truth. If this is told with confidence and with a feeling for the larger meaning of things, it will be better than telling the story of the stork without belief in the truth of the image and thus without the feeling of telling an *un*-truth.

Nevertheless, we must say that the impressive image of a large bird, an earthly apparition despite its high flight, can help the child enter the earthly world more easily than the image of the angel.

Older children who do not "believe" in the stork anymore are usually ready to hear about angels. We can then say that the stork, which we told them about previously, is actually an angelic being.

This being the truth, it will be completely accepted by any healthy, slightly older child, as long as we say it with true conviction.

When the children are older still, we can let them know something about *physical* birth. During adolescence everything is unveiled. The emphasis can now be on the fact that this is *a different side* of the birth process so that the child can experience the two-sidedness and understand that the images he was given as a small child are still true.

## "Cruelty" and other alarming aspects of fairy tales

A different problem that we come across when telling fairy tales is that people are often wary of telling the "cruel" and sometimes "alarming" things that happen in the tales. It is better not to tell these tales if you feel that they *are* "cruel" or "alarming," as your feeling can be transferred to the child. The child might awaken from his image experience to reality, where he does not belong. It is then best if a fairy tale in which such grisly things do not occur is chosen.

With regards to the "cruelties" we should ask ourselves if these are actually cruelties in the language of the fairy tales for the child. Don't forget that the "unpleasant" things in these tales also have image character that essentially excludes all external realism. Let's look at "The Two Brothers" by Jacob Grimm. One of the two brothers (both hunters) has his head chopped off by a godless field marshal while he sleeps. This is very "unpleasant." However, a bit later five animals that work for the field marshal reattach the head and heal the wound with herbs fetched by the hare. Once finished, the animals realize that they have attached the head backwards. So now the lion has to detach the head of his master again after which the mistake is rectified. The healing herbs do their job again and the hunter is healed! It should be clearer than ever that a detached head is nothing "alarming" in a fairy tale. We adults see it realistically, making it a terrible, bloody event. But it means something entirely different for the young child. One can lose one's head much as one can lose the knob of a drawer. There is nothing bloody about it.

Losing one's head in a fairy tale may mean that the character must lose consciousness by day, either temporarily or for good. If we think about this and put ourselves in the understanding of a small child who has no connection with the realistic side of a beheading, we will be able to tell the story passionately, perhaps even with emphasis. It then plays the right part.

Another unpleasant example can be found in "Little Red Riding Hood." If we hear that someone is devoured by a wolf and we don't take into account that a wolf could never devour a whole human being, we imagine a mess of blood and gnawed bones. A child sees this completely differently—grandmother just disappears into the wolf's stomach as if by magic—whoops, she's gone! This is horrible, of course, because it means that the grandmother has disappeared into the kingdom of darkness. Once again, there is no blood, the animal doesn't flinch and just continues sleeping! And then the grandmother and Little Red Riding Hood reappear, not in pieces, but whole and full of life: they return from the kingdom of darkness into the kingdom of light! Stones are then put in the wolf's stomach and he is sewn up so that he will not notice anything when he wakes up. If one thinks of the quality of these images it should be easy to tell them with enthusiasm instead of with feelings of horror or disgust.

However, there are unpleasant events in fairy tales. They show a different aspect—evil that is punished. This punishment can be very cruel, and it is mostly reserved for witches.

Before we go into this further, we should say that some tales that include punishment, such as the witch who was put in a barrel with nails and rolled off the hill (in which we detect something of the medieval origins), should not be told in our time anymore. As punishment, even in the language of images used in fairy tales, we believe they cannot be upheld as they surpass the boundaries of the image and call up feelings in the child that should not be awakened. We would rather transform a punishment such as this into something more acceptable, such as that the witch must serve the young couple that she wanted to injure *for the rest of her life* (see " 'Mother Holle': the conscious world and the dream world" and "For the youngest children: what about happy endings?").

Except for these few examples of images that are not acceptable, we must remember that for the child, evil in fairy tales is not connected to one person, but represents "evil" in general. In "Why do we tell fairy tales to young children?" we saw how good and evil in fairy tales surpasses all our moral boundaries in the broadest sense and actually includes the entire human development from the Fall to conquering it in the future. Thus, an evil being in a fairy tale can also be seen as the personification of specific powers that have helped lead humanity to the Fall, without having to go so far as a barrel with nails. Nevertheless, and for the satisfaction of the child, evil must be overcome or changed into something good.

Punishment in fairy tales often has a meaning in imagery. For example, consider the witch in "Hansel and Gretel." First she lures the children with her house made of cakes and candy. Then she offers them a delightful shelter that can even be digested. Eventually, the boy ends up in a shed behind bars. During the day, when our soul is awake in our body, the body's powers are consumed; the soul "digests" the body—"eats" the body, as it were. If she only does this with enjoyment, the body is "eaten" as if eating cake and candy. In other words, if she allows herself to be tempted by the comforts of life, she will find herself imprisoned in a narrow, rigid materialism (the shed with the bars). In this fairy tale, the witch represents both sides of evil: *temptation* and *rigidity*, the Devil and Satan. Once she has been conquered, her powers must, of course, be disabled radically. She is engulfed by the flames she ignited for her victim. If they have not metamorphosed, the Devil and Satan are eventually consumed by their own powers.

I give myself the liberty to tell a short story about modern thoughts on the above.

I once visited a puppet show of Hansel and Gretel in Rotterdam. The main theme of this performance was love of mankind. In this performance, when Hansel and Gretel returned to their father at the end of the play, their mother was still alive. It would have been too much for the children if they had no longer had a mother! The children told their mother what they had experienced and that they had thrown the witch into the oven. "But," asked the terribly concerned mother, "was the oven on?" "Nooo!" cried Hansel and Gretel together, "Of course not, we just pretended, to scare her!" "Oh, that's good! Otherwise it would have been very bad of the two of you! But now she must be so scared that she'll never do anything like that again!"

I listened and watched, in one eye a smile and in the other a tear.

## About morals in fairy tales and fables

We have seen more than once that the foundations of fairy tales are much broader than everyday moral teachings alone, or than the general terms for good and evil. Young children live strongly in their wills and actions while their thought is still cosmic. They would not be able to understand a direct question about good and evil.

Stories that have conventional morals as their main motive are known as fables. In fables, good triumphs over evil, the wise triumph over fools, and so forth. These triumphs are usually shown in funny or mischievous ways. Fables are especially appropriate for seven- to eight-year-olds—children who have almost completely lost the great cosmic width, the "spiritual memory" (and therefore most of early childhood's fairy tale world), but still prefer to think in images. The will, through which the young child is still completely driven, is now mixed with feelings that actively seek and question morality. Thus, it is understandable that a story that plays on morals and is brought in a humorous way is completely right for this age group. It is therefore a grave mistake that the fables, especially those by La Fontaine[1], are often only read and discussed in high school (by students who consider him boring and stupid). Adolescents, who are searching for the *sensory* world, are no longer interested in these childish intimacies of soul life. On the other hand, children in second grade can become extremely enthusiastic if a fable is told and discussed in an imaginative and fitting manner.

Everyday morals also play an important role in fairy tales. Good is rewarded and evil is punished. However, if the moral is to be fully experienced it should be seen in a much wider context, as we saw when discussing "Mother Holle." But also recall the prince cutting through the hedge in "Sleeping Beauty." The hedge represents moral teachings that rise high above that of the fables.

The vastness of fairy tale morals can sometimes seem to incorporate contradictions to our daily morals. In the world of fairy tales, good and evil can be quite different from what we know in everyday life. Being good parents and teachers who want to teach our children "morality," we may hesitate to give them such "immoral" tales. When posed in such a way, this question seems a bit like the above question about cruelty. However, we mean something completely different with it and hope to clarify this with an example.

The Russian fairy tale "Ivan the Fool" tells of an extremely lazy young man who does nothing but sleep. Ivan is rewarded for his laziness when he catches a pike that gives him magical powers. Ivan gets everything that he wanted. One would think that this would not be very beneficial for children—laziness abundantly rewarded! Everything goes right for Ivan. He tricks everyone and changes himself into a handsome prince who marries the daughter of the king.

Our everyday morals make us look at this story with disapproval, shaking our heads in disgust.

But let's look at how the young child experiences this story. He does not yet understand our everyday morals and still has a dreamy bond with deeper ground. Doesn't his dreamy life protect him from undisclosed spiritual riches and shouldn't he be allowed to dream out his dreams? Won't this give him the magical powers of the fish that lives in pure, ethereal waters: the *spiritual* awakening power of Christianity that will cause him to wake up a "prince," a fully conscious earthly person, full of "I" power?

What wonderful encouragement and reassurance for children who have difficulty waking up out of their dream world. These children will experience an open, deep moral joy and will draw healthy courage for the future when told this tale.

And then there are fairy tales in which cleverness is commended in such a way that honesty may be jeopardized. In these tales, the clever or even sly hero or heroine always wins. In response, we might feel a moral objection. For example, in "Clever Grethel," the main character prepares two chickens for her master, but quietly eats them herself. She bends the truth in such a way that her master blames his guest and drives him out of the house with a knife while she watches with pleasure.

These tales should be seen more as comic stories than fairy tales and should be told to *older* children. They can help seven- to nine-year-olds develop alertness to the relationship between earthly life and audacity! They encourage an audacity that had not become conscious in the people of olden times, who had not yet developed logical thinking. Thus, although a deeper background may be missing, they can still fulfill an important role. They are cheerful incentives for the "lower I," which comes to the fore in our everyday lives, to sometimes dare to try something new—a very good encouragement for this age group. Furthermore, since they are brought as comical jokes about which everyone laughs heartily, there is no danger that the morality of the children is damaged, not even in the external sense. One feels that they originated in a time when this lower "I" needed to be developed and when humanity needed to become conscious to external existence. Even though this necessity no longer exists, as the awakening has already taken place for the most part, these stories remain important not only for their priceless humor but also for developing alertness to audacity in older children.

Connected with morality is the fact that genuine fairy tales are never "solemn." Solemnity is sought when one wants to rise above the everyday mood. A completely healthy young child has not yet descended into an everyday mood and does not know what that is. How could he want to rise above something that he does not know? He is still searching and *must* search for earthly life. This is why fairy tales speak in images of things and beings found in everyday life, as we saw in the previous chapter. Solemnity or sobriety would ask the young child, if he understood it at all, to leave those conquered earthly things behind while they should be the guideposts in his life to come. This is something for adults but not for young children.

In short, solemnity does not belong in fairy tales. This is why even those fairy tales with the deepest content are devoid of solemnity.

There is one point left that would not have been mentioned at all in earlier times but may not be omitted nowadays. This is alertness to today's *truly* substandard stories. There are many people who reject "cruelty" or "immorality" in fairy tales, but do not hesitate to read the children's stories found in newspapers to their young ones. We all know them: "Peanuts," "Donald Duck,"

"Garfield," and so on. We have not even included the graphic novels that let children enjoy crime and all kinds of other things that we would rather not discuss here. This is not about the "goody two shoes" stories that children do not even read because they are so boring. This is about the skillful, even well-written stories that are full of bizarre foolishness or are cleverly sensational, describing all kinds of materialistic events. Children are fascinated by these stories, but they leave child's inner being empty and flat.

Even though they do not contain murder or other crimes, there is no guarantee for the innocence of these stories. Children are naturally interested in images that express a truly great inner life in which their inborn spiritual richness can find a home. The above-mentioned stories reject this, resulting in a development that inevitably becomes materialistic and empty. Later, when the child enters adult life, and he has had a childhood filled with empty nourishment, he will stand shut to the immensity of the world, powerless to affect that which must be controlled or changed—he will be empty. There will be no enthusiasm or light with regard to human ideals; no understanding love of children who are in search of their lives on this earth. What can such a person be for his own children, for his pupils, for the world? And what will become of the world if we all follow this path?

Of course, the dangerous direction the world is taking is not only due to content-deficient stories. Our entire culture is following a path of materialism and technological "progress." All the more reason for every person who prizes the great values in life to help support and develop them wherever possible, especially where children are involved.

---

## ENDNOTES

1 Jean de La Fontaine (1621-1695) was a French fabulist. He is best known for his *Fables*, which became a model for many European fabulists.

# 4 | Some tips for telling fairy tales

In the following chapters, we would like to discuss some more fairy tales and find out what they really want to tell us. The purpose of this book is not to discuss as many fairy tales as possible but to find the right approach and openness to this spiritual message. Even more importantly, we must find the right way to bring this message to those who must receive it: young children.

As educators, we should never be embarrassed. This will only keep us back. Understanding the background of fairy tales can be important but it certainly is not a necessity. Usually one can only see a small part of the background and then everyone sees it from a different point of view. It is much more important to feel a connection with the background; even with those that we *do not* know but for which we only have a gut feeling. In other words, it is about *living* in the fairy tale *atmosphere*. So-called "knowledge of the background" of a fairy tale can hinder, or even abolish this atmosphere, especially if the storyteller thinks he is "there" and his knowledge comes to stand between him and the child. The tale is then told in such a way that it dies. This is the "I know" way. All gained, even "spiritual," knowledge of the background should therefore first be forgotten or be set aside in the mind. Only then will it be possible to dive into the fairy tale atmosphere again and actively give it to the young child.

Only when "knowledge" is developed into a deeper understanding of the tale can it be fruitful for both teller and listener (see "Refrain from explaining the stories").

The best background is that which one discovers on one's own, but only if it is discovered in the right way. If we sit and brood on the deeper meaning of this or that fairy tale and are desperate to know it, in other words if we tackle the tale with our everyday intellect, it will not open itself up to us. Even if we come to discoveries or thoughts that are not completely wrong, it will be difficult to discard the externally simple character and enter into the living inner essence of the tale.

However, if we restrain our urge for knowledge and try to hear what the fairy tale is trying to tell us, it may share its secrets. Do not be disappointed if this takes weeks, months, or even years. If we continue asking with respect and love, the answers will come to us. We will not receive lifeless spiritual concepts, but the quiet secrets will awaken a wonderful inner life in us, a life that will live on in the children. Then the "snow" will fall from Mother Holle's duvet for us and for the children!

Telling the tales themselves can be quite easy, as the images through which their content is expressed speak for themselves. Most importantly, the tale must be told *in its original form*. Personal additions will only obscure the images. Even our own sentiments, for example those we experience when reading a novel, may not be shown while telling the story, as they may lead the young child to something for which he is not yet ready. To express sympathy for the tragic villain who is sentenced to death, or to add a beautiful description of human nature, does not fit in a fairy tale. The images must be presented in their own vivacity. For children past the change of teeth, one can choose stories in which emotions play a larger role, such as the fables. To do this for young children would mean pulling them out of their image experiences. The young child would then skip this part of his development, and suffer an irreparable loss.

This does not mean that we should tell fairy tales without emotion. They must be brought in a *lively* manner. The emotions that one shows should be "objective," they must come from the fairy tale itself with complete *image character*. For example, when a giant speaks, or if we speak about a giant, we can do this with a deep voice, not only because the giant will certainly have a deep voice but also to express the largeness and roughness of the giant's essence. When speaking of a little bird, a light, high voice will be apt. A king will have a strong, assertive voice. This obvious objectivity does not only count for our voice but also for our gestures. These must also originate from the fairy tale. The gestures one makes when speaking about a bear must originate from the weight of the bear. A fawn calls for slenderness, and a lion calls for something different again. Be expressive, making gesture and voice one. In short, one must let the object or character speak for itself: the giant, the bear, the little bird, the king. Another important point is that all these nuances of feeling must be brought in a small way, so that the child's imagination does the rest. If we exaggerate, this soul function will be weakened. If we show too little or no (objective) emotion, then we oblige the child to *understand* the words resulting in a premature awakening effect, depleting and impeding the imagination.

We may feel discouraged by so many suggestions and instructions, but remember that all these suggestions must be *forgotten* once we begin telling the tale, just like our "knowledge" of the background. If we speak from the heart, always keeping the children in mind, we will certainly find the style that fits the children, the fairy tale, and ourselves. We cannot return to previous times, but if we remain concerned that we should find *the* right way to tell the story, then we can find comfort in the fact that hundreds of grandmothers in the past all told the tales differently but all will have told them wonderfully.

## The prince in animal form

### *"The Donkey" (Wilhelm Grimm)*

"The Donkey," by the youngest of the Brothers Grimm, is an especially lively tale about a king and a queen who wanted a child very much but never received one. When they finally did receive a child, a son, it was not a human child but a baby donkey.

After this moving beginning we all secretly hope that the end of the story will reveal a miracle: that the little donkey throws off its hide and a handsome prince appears. And of course, this happens. This is the mystery that sheds its light on the whole story and is concealed in all of us. Don't we all carry this miracle as a concealed possibility within us and are we not destined to actually become a prince or princess in our own right? The "donkey": the drives, urges, instincts (lower beings) that are contained in our physical body can only be refined by our hidden *higher* personality, our *I*, which originated in the spiritual world (a world that has "royal blood"). In other words, our lower being, which covers us like a donkey's hide, can only be discarded by our higher I, our true human being. The latter emerges from the "donkey's hide" as a "prince."

This motif, in which a human child is temporarily bewitched into a different form, only to emerge as his true self later on, appears in many fairy tales. "The Frog King" (or "Iron Henry"), "Ivan the Fool," and "The Swineherd" are good examples. "The Swineherd" depicts a man who must herd his lower instincts (the pigs), and lead them to something good. He is also a prince in disguise. If we look at a gooseherd we see a soul who herds instincts or qualities that already contain the possibility to rise to a higher level. After all, geese are birds, and birds can fly! We could find many other examples. Especially interesting is that St. Francis of Assisi tried to connect with his lower self, with "brother Donkey."

Let's return to the beginning of the fairy tale: The king and queen wanted a child badly but didn't receive one. When one finally did come, it was a baby donkey. We will leave the reaction of the parents aside and first ask ourselves the following question: What does such a longing and long wait mean, and why do they then receive a baby donkey instead of a human child?

Humanity was "thought of" by God and the angels long before it found physical form on earth. Humanity existed in the soul before being born on earth. The process of becoming a physical body had to go slowly so that the human being could be born as a harmonious whole. The hierarchies (God and the angels) who wished for the birth of mankind wisely waited for a long time before granting us earthly bodies. In the language of the fairy tale: the king and queen, who wanted the birth of a human child so much, had to wait for it for a long time.

When mankind first came to live on earth, we were still completely dependent on God. Our true essence, the true human being, had not yet been born. Only when we became distanced from God's leading hand and were forced to create a distance, become independent, would true humanity come to the fore. This is repeated in the life of every child. Every human child would remain a liberated being if she would not become independent from her parents and take her life into her own hands. When this happens, and it certainly does not happen without commotion, the "I" being is born. At a certain age children become difficult and disobedient and often disrespectful towards their parents. Parents are not pleased and usually try to suppress disobedience. They forget that their children can only develop independence through these conflicts. Children must "sin" (be disobedient) towards their parents in this phase of development if they are to enter the world of conscious human beings. Sensible parents do not suppress these difficulties, but lead them towards the right goal: the independence of the child. Once reached, the problems usually stop—the "sins" were needed to reach the goal.

In a larger context, we could say that mankind could not achieve its independence from God without "disobedience." In other words: *the Fall of Mankind was necessary*. In order to become independent, mankind had to follow the path of disobedience temporarily. However, with the Fall, evil entered the world and humanity became subject to all its bad qualities. Speaking in terms of the fairy tale, mankind became a "donkey" through the Fall. This, however, is the beginning of independence, of *true* birth.

Thus, the beginning of the fairy tale actually tells us what the king and queen (the hierarchies) wished for a child: the birth of mankind on earth, for which they had to wait a long time. When a child was finally born (when mankind became an *independent* being on earth), it was a "baby donkey": mankind first became independent as a sinful being (a "donkey") and then became self-conscious, independent, and was truly born on earth.

The fairy tale goes on to say that the queen did not want the child: "I'd rather not have a child than have a baby donkey!" she said. "Let's drown it and be done with it!" But the king says: "No! Even if it is a baby donkey, he is still our son and one day he will be king and sit on my throne!"

This juxtaposes two different principles. For our daily lives, we could divide them as follows: Those of us who do not allow any disobedience or disrespect in their children or students want their children to remain innocent and liberated. They reject the "donkey-form." Like the queen, they want to "drown the donkey." The role of the king lives in those of us who see a real human being in the "donkey," a human being who can and wants to develop into a free and independent person, a human being who wants to mount the throne of self-governance. In the larger context, the queen represents the spiritual powers that do not want to recognize the Fall of Mankind and want to keep mankind innocent as we were before the Fall, thus depriving us of the possibility to develop into free human beings. The king represents those powers that *do* recognize the Fall, the "donkey" being, as the only possibility through which mankind will find *freedom* from the spiritual world and be able to fulfill great tasks on earth *in freedom*.

If we can accept the latter as the truth, then it may become more understandable why God allowed the Fall to happen. We may feel that those of us who want to return to the situation before the Fall want to "undo" this great world drama, ostensibly to pursue a wonderful ideal that is actually against the will of the spiritual world. This does not make sense. If this pursuit is *truly wanted by the spirit,* we will be able to recognize that the consequences of the Fall should be transformed into something good, *the* good for the future, instead of something to undo. We will want to transform the consequences of the fall into the independence of mankind desired by God.

Here is another example. In the East, especially in India, some old connections to specific areas of the spiritual world still exist. Such connections have been lost in the West through the materialism that followed the Fall. Many people in the West are aware of this loss, however this group is divided. Those who cannot tolerate the spiritual loss cannot accept the externalization of Western culture (they want to drown the donkey). They say: "Back to the East, where remnants of the spiritual from before the Fall can still be found!" The other group in the West says: "We see and recognize how much Western civilization has become alienated from the spiritual world. Instead of wanting to return to the East, thus undoing our western externalization, we would rather open up to the spiritual world once again. Despite the narrow-mindedness that our westernization has caused, we want to retain the freedom and independence that our life and knowledge have given us, and develop further." This group tells us: even if Western culture is a donkey, there is a prince hidden in it who will one day mount the throne as a king.

Spiritual science embraces the latter group.

As the fairy tale continues, the little donkey develops well: "His ears grew up straight and tall," in other words, he was a *real* donkey! But at the same time, this being could listen well! He loved music and asked his father for lute lessons. The king brings him to a master in the trade, but is told: "My dear sir, you will never learn this art! Your fingers are too fat! You'll break the strings!" The little donkey does not get discouraged and wants to learn anyway. He practices and practices until he masters the instrument.

Wanting to learn something even though his body does not allow it shows that the little donkey possesses a pure human instinct. No animal will ever want to or be able to learn something other than what its body is capable of: cows will never learn to hunt, lions will never graze in the meadow. However, this little donkey, whose hooves are only fit to stomp and run, wants to learn to play the lute! We begin to sense that there is a human soul hidden in this little donkey! Think of Demosthenes, the great Greek orator, who stuttered as a child, whose speech organs were not fit for speaking. He climbed into the hills with a mouth full of pebbles. Once at the top, he tried to describe the sound of the wind in words and practiced until he had finally learned to control his voice.

The little donkey does the same, defying his master. This master represents those who would teach our children only that for which they show talent and with which they can earn money later in life. Why should they learn something for which they don't show any talent, especially if life doesn't ask it of them? A very practical approach, at least superficially. However, this attitude deprives the child of part of his humanity. Human beings are the only beings on earth that can develop themselves in *all* areas as long as they persist. It is possible that the result of this persistence is hardly perceptible in some areas, but in the far future, perhaps even in a later life, these efforts will flourish and make this person a *true* human being. This last point is extremely important, especially for children with limitations or special needs.

A *human being* carries the seeds of *every* possibility. This is what makes him a *human being*. Our ultimate task is to develop all these possibilities harmoniously, and thus become true human beings. If we lose sight of this goal and allow our children to only develop "in their own way," they will become one-sided, limited, and specialized in a way that is not human but bestial. Animals are "super specialists." Those with hooves are the best at running over the earth, but they cannot climb or creep. Beavers can build beaver homes but they cannot defend themselves. Specialization is not something that will bring us closer to the ideal human being. Many people are proud of the fact that specialization is on the ascendant. However, in its present abstract and extreme form, it is causing us to digress to aspirations that actually belong in the animal kingdom.

It goes without saying that the work that must be done on earth must be divided in tasks. Personal talents and professional competence in various areas is important. We need to find the right social and human balance.

In the same way, we should not pursue a balanced development of the child in a dogmatic or fanatic manner. We need to keep in mind what the child can and cannot do. If we *only* teach him what he cannot do, he will lose confidence and become incapable of doing anything. Humanity has a special task to fulfill on earth with its innate capacities.

In this fairy tale, the little donkey bravely breaks through his animal specialty by acquiring a *new* skill with his clumsy hooves. He breaks free from what the past has dictated, breaks free from the bonds of fate uncovering new possibilities for the future. This is something that does not belong in the animal kingdom, but with humanity. By wanting to and actually learning to play the lute despite his hooves, the little donkey expresses his unconscious desire to be human. This allows him to knock on the gates of humanity (the new castle) later on. He is an example that those of us who have the courage to see ourselves as "donkey-like humans" can follow.

Now that the little donkey knows how to play the lute, he goes for a walk in the woods, absorbed in thought. Humans who have gone through a phase of development become thoughtful and go through a period of internalization. However, few people actually arrive at this stage. Most people avoid being alone with themselves—they look for distractions in fun and entertainment, always looking away. Subconsciously they feel that they may come to difficult discoveries if they were to look at their own soul. However, for those who want to go through an inner development, quiet reflection is a necessity. We don't mean digging around in the soul, complaining about faults or flattering ourselves with our good qualities, but developing a consciousness about what it is to be a human being, a member of humanity who has experienced the Fall of Mankind. We must develop this consciousness through experiencing the possibilities and obligations that are involved with being human. We ask ourselves how we should live with other human beings, how we should do our work, how we should educate ourselves in order to bring light to the darkness of earthly life. Then we are people who are willing to follow this path of development while being in the middle of the "dark trials" of life. We are then willing to stop now and again to ponder, like the little donkey "pondered" in the "dark forest."

The little donkey now arrives at a pond. Bending down to drink, he is confronted with his reflection. For the very first time, he sees that he is a donkey. What a horrible discovery! He no longer wants to stay at home and goes out into the world. Anyone who wants to follow the path we described above will have to go through a horrible discovery at some time. He will have to uncover and confront a horrible monster, his miserable human soul that has digressed from the human ideal. An enormous amount of courage is needed to confront this vision. If we persevere, we will cross a threshold and find entrance to a specific part of the spiritual world.

In some way, we can recognize this threshold in the fairy tale, but in a lighter version. The little donkey sees an ugly animal being and realizes that he is looking at himself. This depresses him so much that he leaves his father's house, taking only one companion with him, probably his guardian angel or maybe the archangel Raphael, the healer, although this is not revealed.

Luckily, he now finds a new castle. "Passing the threshold" leads us out of the "Father-world" (natural life) to a life that demands much more independence and responsibility and in which we will one day find the Son (the "new king").

In the new castle lives a king who has one beautiful daughter. This is our goal! In the world of fairy tales, the "beautiful daughter of the king" represents a pure soul. This royal daughter is a glimpse into the little donkey's future, in other words for the donkey-like human being who wants to purify his soul. Mankind strives towards this future: the little donkey wants to go to the princess! The king of the castle is the father of the princess, in other words, he is the guardian of the little donkey's future, the helper of all donkey-like human beings who strive to purify themselves: the Christ. In the Bible, the new castle, the future of mankind, is called the New Jerusalem. The little donkey, who has had to leave the "world of the Father," who in his youth was carried by God the Father, now arrives in the world of the Son: the healer of sicknesses of the soul, the keeper of mankind's future.

The little donkey knocks on the gate of humanity's future. He knocks with his hooves, his power from the past. No one hears. Then the little creature starts to play the lute; he uses his newly learned ability and this *is* heard! A prayer that is only a request and comes from old powers will not be heard in the spiritual world. However, if it also contains the *will* for something good, something new, it has creative powers and sounds like music to the heavens above. This is answered: the gate to the realm of the future opens.

In the castle the little donkey is shown a place with the servants. "No," he says, "I don't belong here. I am a royal donkey." The little donkey feels that his *I*, that will have to reign over his own lower instincts, is awakening. He no longer wants to remain a servant to these instincts. He is subsequently shown a place among the soldiers. That should be a better place for him, but he feels that he is more of a "king" and wants to sit next to the king. The king understands and laughs saying: "Let the little donkey come to me!" Christ said: "Let the children come to me," in other words, "Let those who are not satisfied with themselves, who are searching for their God-given I and feel like children on this path of development, come to me, for they are the future."

Then the king asks the donkey: "Would you like to wed my daughter?" The donkey turns (it must now look towards the future) and says: "Dear king, your daughter pleases me greatly!" The donkey wants to accept his future. The princess may now sit next to him. The donkey lives happily in the castle for some time. However, he eventually realizes that despite everything, he remains a donkey. This discourages him so much that he wants to go away, go back to his home. Once we have found the right path, progress does not follow right away. Courage is often lost and we want to give up. But the king Christ holds the donkey back, saying: "Everyone here loves you! Your striving soul belongs in the kingdom of the future!"

But then the king puts the donkey to the test. "Do you want lots of gold and silver?" "No, I have enough gold and silver at home." In other words: "I was connected to my golden spiritual fatherland in my youth. However beautiful that was, I do not want to sink back into that old kingdom. I want to go into the future!" "Would you like to govern half my kingdom?" "No, at home I will inherit a whole kingdom!" One day, the lost fatherland will become mine again. Half a future does not belong there! "Would you then like to have my daughter as your wife?" "Ee-haw, ee-haw," exclaims the donkey: that is exactly what he would like to have. His wish is to connect with his future! "Good!" says the king, who loves the donkey and can see his hidden true essence: "Then that is what you will receive!"

The wedding is quickly arranged: the king (Christ) connects this striving soul with its future.

After the wedding, the king commands a servant to spy on the donkey to know how the donkey is behaving himself. The servant sees that the donkey discards his donkey hide just before bed and becomes a handsome prince. When we fall asleep our soul discards our lowly daily worries (our donkey hide). It can then enter the "bed chamber" (the kingdom of the night) in a relatively pure state. When the king hears this, he does not want to believe it at first. The king Christ becomes a normal human being at this point. A strange inconsistency! The Christ, who saw the inner pure essence of the donkey, does not want to believe that this is true. He now looks at it "from a normal point of view."

We should not read too much into this. Fairy tales have been passed on by word of mouth for ages and have lost a lot of their original character. Rudolf Steiner also tells us to distinguish between important things (things that have deeper content) and less important things. I believe we must see this event as a funny psychological game that does not have deeper significance. But it becomes even stranger! The next morning the king sees a happy donkey and asks his daughter if he hasn't made her deeply unhappy by making her marry a donkey. When it turns out she is not, he is very surprised. Think about it: a father who marries his daughter off to a beastly man out of personal sympathy and who is then surprised that his daughter is not unhappy!

Aside from the fact that we should not see the king as Christ-like in these events, there is something else happening here that we talked about before. These fairy tales do not take place in the emotional world of adults. Through their dreamy life and life of the will, they appeal to the world of early childhood. We see this everywhere. One of the biggest flaws of modern fairy tales is that they appeal to the emotions of older children and adults, while they are meant for young children. Real fairy tales speak to us in images, not in emotions!

Let's look at another example. What mother would allow her little daughter to go into the woods at night when she knows that a wolf roams through the forest? Little Red Riding Hood's mother does, and no little child will ever think it strange. The young child only experiences the image of the soul that must enter the darkness.

The same is true in this fairy tale. The king's actions, which would be seen as horrible in any other context, are quite normal in this fairy tale. The images pass by, one by one, without any real emotional consequence. In the end, the king is advised by the servant to see for himself. He slips into the bedroom at night and takes the donkey hide. This event gives the king something of the Christ back, even though it is a very human act. Christ also comes to us silently, like a "thief in the night." This may surprise us but it is true. Today, when we speak of Christ in big words or believe that we can connect with Him through visualizing Him, we are actually as far from Him as possible. It is during quiet moments, when we have turned inward, or when we enter the spiritual realm of the night, that He can "slip in" unnoticed. This can happen to anyone even though we don't remember anything that happened the next day. More highly developed people can receive these gifts more consciously than others. Goethe could sometimes wake up with a thought or poem that he felt was a gift during the night. He had to write it down immediately so as not to lose it and had great respect for these nightly "gifts."

A great step has been made if we can experience these spiritual inspirations while conscious during the day. In the end, man can open himself in such a way that he becomes a servant and representative of the spiritual world for other people. Moses was such a person. However, this level of development brings great responsibility. Moses's people depended on him, and when he doubted God's word he was severely punished. Those of us who are not ready are put off by the responsibility. This is also seen in the fairy tale. The prince was used to wearing his donkey hide during the day. In other words, he could be a "normal" donkey person without great responsibilities. Suddenly, his hide was taken away. The king had it burned. Now the prince had to be a "prince" during the day as well, a radiant representative of the spirit for mankind. This was too much for him, and he wanted to flee back to his father's home: he wanted to go back in his development. The king, once again in his role as Christ, holds him back for a second time and awakens his courage to fulfill the tasks that his future holds for him.

Think of the raising of Lazarus. In the same way as Christ woke Lazarus back to life from his seeming death, during which he was connected to the spirit, the king calls the prince out of his nightly spiritual experience into the consciousness of day. By burning the donkey hide, he forces the prince to be a prince during the day as well. He forces him to be a radiant spiritual human being.

The fairy tale ends when the prince becomes king and reigns over two kingdoms: that of his own father and that of the princess's father. A human being, as a fully conscious spiritual servant in the world reigning in the present, stands in two worlds: the past and the future.

Thus, this fairy tale shows us the path of spiritual development of mankind through many trials and experiences, from the Fall to the final victory, or "healing": the New Jerusalem.

### *"The Frog Prince" or "Iron Henry" (Jacob Grimm)*

Let's now compare "The Donkey" to the well-known fairy tale "The Frog Prince" or "Iron Henry." One of the most notable differences between these two tales is the length. "The Frog Prince" is short and powerful compared to "The Donkey. " This is partly due to the different styles of Jacob and Wilhelm Grimm. However, the contrasting temperaments of the two protagonists also plays a part. The frog is a phlegmatic creature that arouses disgust in the princess, who then throws him about. The donkey is a melancholic who must work through much darkness in himself, a process that takes quite some time, even in the fairy tale.

Aside from these differences, there is also a telling similarity. Both fairy tales involve a prince disguised as an animal. This is what we would like to look into now.

In the previous fairy tales, we discussed what we can see in the prince who often heroically frees the princess, who awakens her from her dreams. He represents another prince, the "prince" that we all carry within us but who has not or has only partially shown himself to us. This is our higher spiritual origin, our "I" being. This higher I being is not yet ready to reign over our lower being: not yet a king, it is still a prince. But as in the fairy tale where the prince is destined to free the princess and become king, the prince *within us* is called to awaken and free *our* princess (our soul with all its emotions and longings) from her bondage and take her to his kingdom (the spiritual world). Here they will become king and queen, in other words they will reign over their own essence and collaborate in the development of the earth that surrounds them.

Why does the prince manifest in the form of an animal?

We all know from experience that the most important people in life can also often be the most difficult. They have great qualities and possibilities, but their "I" from which these are born is not yet ready to govern and lead them. This is why these strong but insufficiently controlled qualities often cannot or can only partially find their way in this strange (for them) earthly world to which the physical body belongs. The consequence is extreme stress that can express itself in all kinds of excesses or misbehavior. Thus, a positive characteristic or valuable virtue can be a severe imbalance or an extreme vice in the physical world. A born leader can appear to be a tyrant before he gains control over his powers. A potentially great artist can overreact through his emotions. "The bigger the spirit, the bigger the beast" (*Hoe groter geest, hoe groter beest*), say the Dutch. One day, when a group of people were out walking with Rudolf Steiner and came across a drunkard, they looked at the man in disgust. Dr. Steiner then said that this man had the biggest personality of them all. Cornelis Winkler, a professor of psychology from the early twentieth century, once personally told me: "If I hadn't become a professor I would have become a criminal."

There are many more examples.

Of course, the saying above is only valid to a certain point. Those who can develop to an even higher degree can become even more balanced and stronger leaders of their lower being. Then the prince discards his donkey hide and becomes king.

A special light is shed on such soul life imbalances when we look at the figure of Michael. Michael is not only the angel of the sword but also the angel of the scales. He teaches our I to fight, but he also teaches us to weigh things in our souls. First of all, we need to learn to weigh what is really important in life. This can be hidden in small things that seem so trivial that we would not notice them if Michael hadn't taught us how to weigh them. Other things that seem very important push to the fore in such a way that we are inclined to become completely caught up in them, thus hiding the things that are actually important. There was once a young man who was destined to become a great violinist. He was ambitious and egocentric. He had an accident, lost a finger, and had to give up his dream. He now had to give lessons to earn his keep. Many people took pity on him throughout his life, but a few of them saw that this man, through his personal disposition, would have lost himself in vanity as a famous violinist. He now had to turn his attention to others, allowing the first signs of the love of mankind to become conscious. Even fewer people saw the value of the awakening of this seed of love compared to the radiance that would otherwise have surrounded him and would have eaten away his heart.

Michael also teaches us to develop in a well-balanced way the possibilities and qualities that slumber within us. If we weigh something that is small, small weights are used on the scales and it is not difficult to find the right balance. If the balance is disturbed, it can easily be found again. But if something large is weighed and large weights are used, keeping balance will ask for much effort and when lost, the scales will dip fiercely. The same is true for human beings. For someone with few possibilities it will not be difficult to spend life as a good and honest citizen. However, if someone has great possibilities that are not kept balanced by fate, it will be a weighty task to find the right harmony. He will have conflicts and stress that can throw him completely off balance: one side of the scales rises high while the other sinks into the depths. Thus, someone with a lot of soul power can achieve great, maybe even brilliant forms of expression while at the same time doing ignoble things. This can surprise decent people who have ordinary capabilities. They may even find it shameful, but they forget that they owe their balance largely to their limited capacity. Once the others learn to weigh their souls according to what Michael taught us, they can become leaders in the development of mankind. If we educate ourselves spiritually, this is possible for each and every one of us.

In order to form an impression of different types of people and different human qualities, let's now look at the essences of the donkey and the frog.

We know the donkey as being a stubborn animal. However, in the East, for example in Israel, it is highly regarded as an indispensable companion to human beings. Because of its tolerance and its willingness to serve, it is sometimes called "the Christian among animals." Its perseverance is seen as "positive stubbornness." Another attractive characteristic of the donkey is its melancholic temperament, as we already mentioned above. When we hear a donkey bray it sounds as if all the world's grief flows through it. A passionate sob shakes his entire body, culminating in the howling sound that we call braying. If we learn to understand the sounds that animals make, we may be able to awaken a consciousness for our task as helper of the beings of nature that have been put in our trust. We will then also learn how every animal being reflects a part of our own being, but magnified (see the previous chapter). This is exactly what the animals in fairy tales do. We saw how the donkey reflects the melancholic human being in the previous fairy tale, not only in a personal but also in a much broader sense. The donkey actually shows us an image of all mankind that must learn to deal with and carry the heavy, dark consequences of the Fall. Humanity recognizes how far it has sunk and becomes just as sorrowful as the donkey was when he saw his donkey face reflected in the pond. But just as the donkey in the fairy tale stubbornly persists in finding his way in life until he can finally rid himself of his hide, we must learn to persevere in the development that lies before us.

The frog expresses a completely different side of human soul life. A frog is a strange, many-sided animal that we can look at in many different ways. In fairy tales, it is often seen as a wise being even though when looking at it, we only see a small, cute little thing that cockily holds its head high as if any comment will slide off its slippery back. But at the same time, it is a bit "dirty." It is strange to learn that spiritual science has us see frogs and toads as the "excrement of the earth." We think excrement is dirty but we should never forget that we have fresh bread every day thanks to excrement. How would a farmer ever harvest wheat if he did not fertilize his fields? Even today's artificial fertilizers originated due to the need for nourishment of the earth.

In some fairy tales, the frog and toad play a double role. A Grimm tale tells of a child who becomes friends with a toad ("Märchen von der Unke," unfortunately translated as "Stories about Snakes"). Her mother thinks the toad is dirty and kills it. Now the child dies too, just like wheat in an unfertilized field: it has been robbed of its spiritual soil.[1]

We can see the "dirty" and "stubborn" side of the frog from a positive angle. True wisdom is loathed and rejected by those who cannot bear it. When we hear a wise man speak, our reaction is often disgust and denial. But if he is truly wise he will not take the slightest notice of this. Just like the frog, he lets ridicule and contempt "slide off his back" and continues to say what he must. Thus is the frog the carrier of a certain degree of wisdom in many fairy tales.

There is something else that is even more important. The frog is a citizen of two worlds. It lives in the world of silent fish, in the water, but at the same time it is one of us, living and breathing on the earth. All great wise men also live in two worlds. They breathe with us in our earthly environment, but they also sojourn in the world of the spirit. The frog originates in a pond; the wise man comes and speaks to us from the world sea of the spirit and can reveal great secrets from that unreachable realm.

However, the wisdom of the frog has another hidden nature. It withdraws into depths and darkness where the wise man lifts himself with his spirit. Through its unpleasant, unearthly appearance in which the divine idea nevertheless lives, the frog's concealed wisdom is even deeper and more mysterious.

The same type of divine wisdom is found concealed in the insignificant form of an earthworm. This small animal lives in the womb of the earth and is basically seen as a revolting being that eats its way through the dirt. Through its work, the earth becomes fertile. Once again, as we saw with excrement, we should thank the earthworm for a good deal of our life on earth. Both excrement and the earthworm can be seen as manifestations of a deeply concealed but no less great wisdom that brings us what we need, regardless of our disgust.

In this sense, our conscience is also a "wise man." We think that whatever the "gnawing earthworm" tells us is unpleasant and if we notice that it touches our feeling of self-respect, we consider it discreditable and ridiculous. Our conscience is our "higher I" that speaks to our "lower I." The former, that part of us that in some hidden way is still in connection with our divine origin, tells our lower I what is truly good and correct. But our lower I, our daily self that is out to find ease, honor, and benefit, resists in every possible way. Not until it has gone through conscious self-development can it finally open its ears to hear what the higher I has to say.

The frog represents all of the above in the fairy tale "The Frog Prince." In the tale, the human soul (the princess) meets her still-enchanted higher I (the frog). This small being can return the lost golden ball (of which we will soon learn the meaning) to her. However, the soul does not stay loyal to the I. The soul walks away and doesn't want to hear the voice of the I (the conscience). The I knocks again and again and keeps talking until the soul finally listens and obeys. Only then can the marriage between the soul and the higher I take place (the initiation of the soul in the spiritual world).

Now that we have looked at the main characters of this story and have seen how they are connected, we will try and let the story speak to us through its great images.

"The Frog Prince" or "Iron Henry" is about a king who has many beautiful daughters. The youngest is so beautiful that even the sun is surprised each time it shines on her face. The rest of the fairy tale is about this daughter. The other daughters are no longer mentioned.

The human soul that originates in the Father world develops into an ever higher and more beautiful consciousness. Consequently, the youngest phase of the soul's development (the youngest daughter) must be the most beautiful and important.

The fairy tale tells about this youngest daughter and how much she loves to go into the woods surrounding her father's castle. One day she goes into the woods to play with her golden ball. Even our youngest "soul daughter" yearns for consciousness and likes to leave her bright origins to go into the darkness of earthly life. Here she searches for her inner development. Entering the darkness reminds this soul daughter (however concealed) of the brilliant spiritual world from which she came. With this experience of her origins, of the radiant cosmos, the "golden ball," she enters the darkness. She plays with the radiant ball in the forest. Originally the soul lived and played in the "golden cosmos." She has had to leave this cosmos and now plays *with,* not *in,* this "golden ball." She throws it up and catches it, again and again. That is what the awakening consciousness on earth that no longer lives *in* the spirit does: it plays *with* the spirit, it rejects it and searches for it again.

But then the ball falls on the ground and rolls into a deep well. Consciousness has now completely lost its connection with the spiritual world. Spiritual life has become completely worldly: it has "sunk into the earth."

This process, which occurs in every child's life, is masterfully and beautifully told in Frederik van Eeden's "Kleine Johannes" ("Little John"). Little John, who plays in the dunes and understands the language of animals and plants, still lives in the world of the Father. At a certain point, he meets a gnome called "Wist ik" (literally, "Knew It"). The gnome lets him see the world in a totally different way, from the viewpoint of longing for external knowledge. Little John must now leave his life in the golden spiritual world and live a sober, external and materialistic earthly life. He quickly meets another being that brings him even further into the darkness: the little demon "Pluizer" ("Scrutinizer" or "Unraveller"). Little John makes Pluizer unravel the greatest problems so that he can increase his external knowledge.

In the fairy tale, we see the same loss of the Father world: the ball rolls into a well and sinks into the depths before the eyes of the princess. The soul of mankind is absorbed into the "womb of the earth." It must become one with the earth.

But the well is filled with water! The ball does not fall onto the dead hardness of the earth, into a grave, but into flowing, living water.

Water has always been seen as the life-carrying element of the earth. The Germanic people saw the world as a giant and the seas and rivers as his flowing blood. In the plant world, water, in the form of rising fluids, carries growth and life forces. The fact that the ball falls into the life element of the earth can be seen as an expression of the fact that the spiritual world has not just "ossified into earth" but has found new life in the earthly realm. Everything that lives on earth actually expresses the life of the spirit. This life should not only be seen in the literal sense, but also in colors, forms, and sounds. A small child recognizes the inner life of the spirit that has transformed into earthly things in all these things and beings: in an opening bud, a growing plant, a flower, butterfly, bird or other animal; but also in colorful stones, the voice of the wind, the song of birds. We could say that the spirit presents itself in "enchanted" form in the above. Everything that the child sees around him on earth reminds him (mostly unconsciously) of the "enchanted" form of something that he carries deep within, given to him before birth in the spiritual world. We have already spoken about this.

However, this unconscious knowledge fades, becoming weaker and weaker until it is almost completely gone: the golden ball sinks so deep that the princess considers it lost. The soul no longer "recognizes" the essence of things, looking *at* things as we adults almost always do. How can we rediscover the spirit that is concealed in earthly things ("enchanted")?

Our soul powers cannot do this on their own. Neither can our intellect. We need to apply a higher principle of the spirit in us, our "I being." Our soul powers can only develop when led by this higher principle. Only then will they be able to recognize the living spirit in its "enchanted" form and only then will the soul again become a citizen of the spiritual world. In order to achieve this, we must follow a conscious path of spiritual education, led by our higher I, that in turn is inspired by higher powers. What such a path of development asks of us is often difficult and sometimes even unpleasant. We therefore often tend to decline these demands with disgust.

In the fairy tale, this is wonderfully portrayed in the encounter between the princess and the frog.

As the princess grieves for her lost ball, a frog emerges from the well and asks what she would give him if he were to retrieve the ball for her. The princess offers him all kinds of riches, but the frog declines them: "I don't need gold and silver," he says, "but if I can be your best friend and can play with you all day, I will retrieve the ball for you."

Many people try to fill the void of the lost spiritual world with earthly riches. However, this "gold and silver" will never be able to replace what has been lost. Therefore, our deeper being, our I, declines it. Even higher knowledge and intellect, which so many people pursue to enrich their "spirit," does nothing. Only our higher I, which is actually a part of the spiritual world, can uncover it for us again. And this can only happen if the soul listens to the whispers of our I being. What the I has to tell us usually gets lost in the noise of daily life. We need to have intimate contact with our I in order to hear what it has to say. Our higher being must become "best friends" with our soul if its silent words are to be understood. Only then can the spiritual world be rediscovered.

The princess promises the frog her friendship, but thinks to herself: a frog can never become the friend of a human child. Our soul does the same thing when it decides to listen to the I's whispers, when it decides to follow the path of spiritual education. Even if the decision is made sincerely, she will still think: "It won't come to that. If it gets too difficult, I can always pull out." However, the frog (the I) takes the princess's promise seriously and dives into the well. The I can dive very deep, it can also submerge itself into things (it can go into things deeply) and can thus rediscover the original essence of things.

We saw the same polarity between depths and heights in the fairy tale "Mother Holle," in which the girl descends into the well only to find the higher spiritual world in its depths. And later on in the tale, she lets it "snow" on earth.

Soon the frog brings the golden ball back to the princess. This may surprise us. We can't possibly just reconnect with the spiritual world when we decide to follow the path of spiritual education!

On the contrary, one could say that as soon as the decision is made in earnest, we can feel the deeper connection with the spiritual world even though we cannot actually see it consciously yet. It is almost as if we are allowed to hold the "golden ball."

Moreover, time is relative in fairy tales. For example, a princess who may be seven years old marries a prince the next day. Sleeping Beauty slept one hundred years before she was woken up by her prince. Time has image character in the latter example. In the former the images are simply put next to each other and time plays no part. Thus, we should not be surprised that retrieving the "golden ball," a process that takes years and involves many trials, happens quickly in this tale.

Once the princess has her precious object back, she forgets her promise and runs home, even as the frog calls after her. The family is at dinner in her father's castle; one could say that they are partaking in the "meal of life." The princess is also at the table. The soul takes in what life, given to her by the Father, brings. Then she hears splat, splat, splat on the marble steps outside. The voice of conscience! Our conscience does not always speak with clear words, but begins with a murmur. There is a knock on the door. The princess opens the door but quickly slams it shut when she sees the frog. However, she must now tell her father, our royal Father (the soul must confess), what is happening. He demands that she keep her promise, just as God requires us to keep our promises. She must now take the frog beside her and he must actually become her "best friend." He is even allowed to eat from her plate! The soul must allow the I to eat with it at the table of life; the I must play a role in our life.

But now the princess is disgusted with the food.

This happens so often. When the I interferes, in other words when we achieve a higher consciousness, the natural connection with things temporarily disappears. When the young Rudolf Steiner was editor of a well-known magazine and published various revelations of the conscience, subscription after subscription was cancelled. People could not bear such revelations. Something similar happened to a conductor of the Utrecht Orchestra. When he discussed the background of the music they were going to rehearse, many musicians complained that they lost their joy of playing. You can only understand and bear such consciousness if you have reached a certain a level of development. Only then will the joy be increased instead of lessened. The same happens to the princess. When the frog ate from her plate, she lost her appetite.

Finally she goes to her bedroom. The frog wants to accompany her, just as the I wants to connect with the soul in the transcendental realm of the night. The initiation into the world of the spirit must take place. The princess resists at first. She puts the frog in the corner of the room. This is also often seen in life. So often when the time is ripe for something new in our lives, we resist. Let's look at pre-puberty. In the phase just before girls and boys start to be attracted to each other, they are the cruelest to each other. But we also see this resistance to something new in adults. Just before Joost van den Vondel, a Dutch writer and poet, became a Catholic, he wrote poems attacking the Catholic church. His deeper self already felt a connection with the church, but his daily consciousness, which also took into account the reproaches he would have to endure, could not yet take the step. He had always been known as an advocate of Protestantism. In order to suppress this inability, he attacked the Catholic church, putting the frog (his higher consciousness) "in the corner of the room."

In the fairy tale, the frog persists and the princess becomes so angry that she throws the frog against the wall. This act breaks the spell and the prince, in all his glory, now stands before her.

Here is another surprise: a fierce tantrum is rewarded with something beautiful!

We should now note that in the original version of this fairy tale, the princess actually takes the frog into her bed, and while in bed the frog changes into a prince: the soul connects with the manifested I.

Of course, a young child would not see any eroticism in this, but would only experience it as an *image*. However, Jacob Grimm seems to have thought that the frog in bed with the princess, especially in the eyes of adults, was not fit for children. But the first version clearly has a deeper meaning. Remember that the soul doesn't react towards the I itself, but to its enchanted form. If we look at it from a positive perspective, we could say that the soul could no longer stand the I being enchanted, and became so angry that it (unconsciously) broke the I's bonds. Sometimes enormously strong actions in life are needed when the I cannot achieve the necessary freedom of the soul. An extreme act of the soul can then sometimes free the I from captivity. Thus, we see that the path of a choleric can be very different from that of a melancholic. The melancholic "donkey" in the previous fairy tale quietly doffed his donkey hide at night. The choleric princess smacks the frog against the wall during a tantrum.

Destiny, which aims to allow the soul to follow its designated course, can present itself in many different ways. It can cause the soul to experience silent, deep events, but it can also cause it to experience intense shocks and difficult trials.

When the prince appears, he tells the princess that a witch enchanted him and that she alone (the princess) can release him from this spell. The same is true for all of us. On earth, the I can only present itself to us in "enchanted" form: it cannot show itself in all its greatness. A spell has been put on it by the "witch" (earthly life), a spell that can only be broken if the "princess" (our soul) is truly prepared to give herself.

We should not forget that both the prince and the princess, which appear as two different characters in the fairy tale, both exist within ourselves. This strange phenomenon is seen in all fairy tales. The little girl in "Little Red Riding Hood" represents something of our soul—but so do the grandmother and the mother, the hunter and even the wolf. All these beings can be found within us. We could say that if we were to turn our soul inside out while engrossed in a good fairy tale, we would observe all the characters and figures in the tale projected around us. Thus, the words spoken by the prince to the princess are words that our own I says to our soul.

The wedding is quickly arranged. The profound connection between the I and the soul, the "initiation" giving access to the spiritual world, takes place.

A carriage from the prince's fatherland now appears, ready to take the royal couple to the castle. The horses are adorned with plumes. In "Hansel and Gretel" the children are carried over the water by a white duck (sometimes a white swan) in order to reach their father's home. After all the trials that the "witch" put them through, they are carried across the river by the spirit (the white-feathered bird); the river is the border between them and the world of the Father. In the present fairy tale, the white-plumed horses represent the quick, light tread of the spirit that brings us to our home in the world of the Father, whence we all come and to which we must all return.

Loyal Henry, who was so sad to have lost his master, stands on the back of the carriage. He has come to collect his master. He is the servant who comes to "carry" his master and mistress in the carriage, much as our physical body "carries" our spirit and soul through earthly life!

However, our physical body, the sheath surrounding our soul and spirit, is actually threefold. The physical substance—mineral, just like any stone—is permeated by life forces contained in a "life body," a trait we share with plants. Our feelings, thoughts, and will form yet another organic whole that makes up the third sheath of the soul and spirit. These three sheaths or bodies are led and led by our I being, the sheath from which our soul functions come. Without this leadership, we could never be truly human. If we were to cut off our I and submit to our fancies and instincts (which can also lie in the area of the intellect), we would run wild or become bestial. The second sheath, the "life body," would become overrun without leadership, much like a tropical plant in fertile soil. It would "overrun" the "space" that the spirit needs. The physical body would deteriorate in another way, something that we sometimes see in people who have somehow lost part or all of their spirit, such as people who have temporarily lost themselves emotionally, or have become mentally ill, causing bodily distortions or degeneration.

Our threefold sheaths can thus derail in a threefold way if they are not governed by the I. Therefore, loyal Henry has three iron bands welded around his heart. These bands were placed around his heart to ensure that it would not "burst" without the leadership of his master. But now these bonds have become superfluous and they burst one by one through pure joy. As soon as the true leader arrives once again, bondage can cease to exist.

The couple, prince and princess, go to the father's castle and soon become king and queen. The human being initiated in the spirit (as servant of the spirit) becomes co-creator and co-ruler of that which happens in the world.

## The "three sisters and three brothers" motif

In the last fairy tale, we saw how the youngest daughter of a king represents the ever-deepening conscious development of the human soul. In many other fairy tales, this is portrayed in three phases, or three soul areas. Spiritual science defines three main phases of development of the soul, both in each individual's life and in humanity as a whole. These three soul levels are called the sentient soul, the intellectual soul, and the consciousness soul. The consciousness soul, the "youngest" of the three, is destined to include the I consciousness. In this sense, it is also the most important, just as the "youngest" are often the most important in fairy tales. Through her youth and purity, the youngest daughter is also the "fairest" of the three. However, because of her youthfulness she also seems inexperienced and clumsy compared to her older and more developed "soul sisters," so they look down on her. Thus we arrive at the well-known Cinderella motif. In this fairy tale, there are also three sisters. The youngest is the fairest but also the least significant and (apparently) the least intelligent. She is mocked and bullied by her two older sisters, who misuse her servitude. However, in the end it is Cinderella who marries the prince and becomes queen. In other words, Cinderella stands for the rising I spirit.

If there are three brothers in a fairy tale, the youngest is usually the dreamiest or least intelligent, and he is disregarded by his older brothers. But in the end, he accomplishes the greatest deeds and becomes king. If we look at this as the three brother motif, it might seem that it has to do with what actively comes from the soul, the *functions* of the soul, instead of with the soul itself and its phases of development. Everyone who works with children knows that those who have not gone through the change of teeth live completely by the impulses of the will. Not until elementary school does the feeling life play a more important and subtle role. From adolescence onward, thinking becomes increasingly exact. The soul functions of mankind—willing, feeling, and thinking—develop in exactly that order. In the beginning, mankind acted from the will of the soul, still visible in some primitive cultures. Today, living completely from the will is seen as decadent and even demonic, approaching a tendency to running wild. An unbridled will becomes wild. This is why people from primitive cultures are often seen as "wild men." However, people in ancient civilizations received their will impulses directly from the spiritual world. Living from the will was completely carried by the spirit and was the highest form of this early soul function. Not until much later did feeling come forward. Because of its more recent development, feeling is closer to us than willing. We can visualize this by thinking of the life of the artist or craftsman in medieval times. It was not until recent centuries that logical thinking developed in science and technology. However, logical thought in its present state of development is barren and uninspired. It is still only a human creation, lacking the depth that comes from the higher powers present in willing and feeling. Thinking, the "youngest brother" of the three soul functions, cannot yet play an essential part in the subtler sides or deeper layers of cultural life. It is too systematic and angular. It must remain with its "older brothers," willing and feeling, until it has attained the missing inner life. Once thinking has awakened to true inner life, it will become the most cultured of the soul functions. Then it will become "king" of the soul life and reign over culture and the development of mankind.

In most fairy tales, we see either the male element, such as the three brothers of whom the youngest marries the princess, or the female element, as in "Cinderella." Rarely are both elements together in one tale, except in stories such as "Hansel and Gretel" and "Little Brother and Little Sister." In these tales, the soul and the I go down the path of life hand in hand. However, it is not the "higher I," our true I, that leads the soul but its earthly reflection, our "lower I," which starts emerging early in life. It still must pass many tests before it can become one with its spiritual origins, the "higher I." Think of Hansel, whom the witch has put in a cage so that she can throw him into the fire later on, or "Little Brother" and everything he has to go through in the tale that we will discuss next. It is interesting to see that the boy must experience the worst events in both tales. The girl (the soul) stays by her brother's side (the lower I) and takes care of him.

Let's now look at "Little Brother and Little Sister." Just as in "Hansel and Gretel," "Tom Thumb," and all fairy tales of this type, life is not pleasant for the children at home. Eventually, they must leave their parental home. In "Tom Thumb" and "Hansel and Gretel," the children are misled by the parents and left in the forest. In "Little Brother and Little Sister," the children decide to run away themselves. The difference is not so great because in all the tales, the children are forced to flee their sad destiny. Mothers have died, stepmothers have arrived, and life has become unbearable at home. "Long ago, when mother was still alive, life was good," they grumble, "but our stepmother doesn't even give us a crust of dry bread! We can just as well look for food in the forest!" And that is what they do.

Let's look more closely at the "evil stepmother," a phenomenon that is often seen in fairy tales and is quite a controversial theme today.

We have already seen the evil stepmother in "Mother Holle": the sweet, beautiful girl is the stepdaughter of the widow. The pure human soul is the "stepchild" of "Widow Earth," who keeps her riches from this soul that wants to develop spiritually; she is the "stepmother" to this soul. The same is the case in "Little Brother and Little Sister." Understandably, our modern, humane society must reject this abusive and discouraging motif. There will certainly be some fathers who will feel embarrassed by these fairy tales if they hear them being told by the mother. In the tales, it is often the father who is loving towards the children while the mother, who may not actually be a stepmother, is nasty and greedy and does not give the children any attention. Doesn't this give the children the wrong impression? Won't this cause them to see an "evil stepmother" in every stepmother they may encounter?

These objections, while logical and understandable, have only arisen because we adults have almost completely lost our ability to see and comprehend images. Our adult objections do not belong in the soul world of the young child. We have forced our adult world on the children via education. Even Maria Montessori felt that the images conjured up by fairy tales were "made up," a belief that I like to call the "psychological iconoclasm of Montesorri."

If a young child is healthy, these fairy tale motifs can be none other than images of larger things that she subconsciously carries within. Experiencing the image of the great "Father" who loves all his children or the great "Mother Earth" who has become our "stepmother" since the Fall will not diminish the love she and her mother feel for each other at all. The world of fairy tales is a *world of images* that speaks to the child in a different way than logical, objective reality.

Furthermore, the word "stepmother" is only a collection of sounds for the young child. The word "mother" is preceded by the sound "step," which sounds a bit like "stiff." A small child is not yet conscious of the real meaning of the word "stepmother," unless she is very precocious. Furthermore, she will most likely not even know which women in her surroundings are stepmothers. By the time she knows what a "stepmother" is and actually meets one, she will know how to distinguish (although maybe not consciously) between the outside world and the inner language of fairy tale images.

It may well be that when a more grown-up child consciously meets a real live stepmother for the first time, he may be surprised how different she is from the ones he encountered in fairy tales. She may even be nice and loving instead of nasty and cruel! A healthy reaction would not be: "She should be cruel because that's what I've always heard in the fairy tales," but: "What I now encounter in the real world, speaks to me *differently* than the fairy tales did." Therefore the stepmother will be given a clean slate! If the circumstances are healthy, this process happens very quickly.

Indeed, the reaction is often the opposite of what people expect. If a child arrives at a logical, conscious, external observation during pre-adolescence and adolescence, his new experiences will not be judged based on his earlier image experiences. He will look at the dream world that he only recently left behind with his newly discovered logic. In most cases the dream world vanishes like snow in the sun, or is called "a nice fib," or even "pure nonsense."

This should not be seen as a problem, although we may feel it is "tragic." In a larger context, all mankind experienced this tragedy when we left paradise in order to meet the outside world. And what was experienced by all mankind must be re-experienced by each person individually. Looking towards the future, we could say that we are at the brink of change: in the same way that every person has the possibility to rediscover the lost spiritual world in later life, all mankind, whose consciousness is enriched by endless trials, will one day be allowed to enter the "New Jerusalem." In the same way, once a child has come to the right age he must experience his own tragedy and learn that he too can achieve this higher consciousness through his own actions.

Let's get back to our initial question. We believe that we should leave behind our humanistic scruples that completely lack any kind of image content, even though we would love to defend the plight of real stepmothers. For the young child, it will be best if we just tell the part of the tale that has to do with the "evil stepmother" in a fitting way even if the possibility exists that we ourselves are a stepmother, but then of course a loving, caring one!

Now that we have discussed this controversial subject, we can return to the fairy tale "Little Brother and Little Sister." The children, complaining about the terrible care that they get from their stepmother, decide to run away into the dark forest. We could also say: after having lost the connection with the "World" or the father, and seeing Mother Earth become a widow, humanity ends up in the dark.

In the forest, Little Brother and Little Sister find shelter in a hollow tree trunk. The trunk of a tree, unlike the tree's young twigs, buds, and flowers, has actually more or less become part of the earth again. Even more so if the trunk is dead. Seeking shelter in a hollow tree trunk can thus almost be seen as taking shelter in the depths of the earth. In other words, the children completely connect with the earth that has become so dark for them. they accept their sad fate.

Morning comes. Little Brother is very thirsty so they go to look for a spring. Little Brother, the male element of humanity, "thirsts" for what the earth has in store for him. Our lower "I" wants to feast upon the source of earthly knowledge and earthly goods. But mankind has lost its relationship with earth since the Fall. We are egotistical and only want to benefit from what the earth has to offer, which in a way "poisons" our development as human beings. If we look at this differently we could say: when Mother Earth became stepmother to mankind after the Fall, all her springs were poisoned. Those who are driven by lust and drink from the poisoned springs will develop in a less than human, even bestial manner. In the fairy tale, we now discover that the stepmother, who is actually a witch, has secretly poisoned all the springs so thirsty Little Brother cannot quench his thirst.

When the little boy wants to drink out of the first spring, his sister hears the water whisper, "Whoever drinks from me will turn into a tiger; whoever drinks from me will turn into a tiger!" and she is able to keep him from drinking. The soul, that will one day be governed by the higher I, must first lead the lower I through life despite its instincts and lusts. She must control his cravings and keep him from becoming bestial.

At the second spring, the water whispers: "Whoever drinks from me, will turn into a wolf; whoever drinks from me, will turn into a wolf!" and again Little Sister is able to hold him back.

At the third spring, the water whispers, "Whoever drinks from me will turn into a deer; whoever drinks from me will turn into a deer!" Little Brother can no longer control himself. He drinks, and turns into a fawn.

While discussing "The Little Donkey," we spoke about the developing human souls that could not live on earth in the beginning of the earth's development. They had to wait for the right time before their "descent" could be harmoniously achieved. Those souls that could not wait, descended in a haphazard way causing them to shoot in all directions and run aground in their development. This is how the animals were created—beings that wandered off the main path of humanity and, in their one-sidedness, reached the end of their development.

The beings who wandered off first, who "drank" from the earthly "springs" first, became the wildest and least human. Think of the dinosaurs in the prehistoric world. In fairy tales, we cannot speak about prehistoric animals. Therefore, the most vicious animal is the tiger. Little Brother endured the threat of becoming a tiger. Drinking out of the second spring would have had a less wild effect: the wolf! However, he is able to conquer that hazard as well. At the third spring, he is no longer able to contain himself, drinks, and becomes a fawn.

Even the souls that were able to contain themselves until life on earth was possible for mankind were not completely balanced. They also had their one-sidedness, their bestial side, even though they were able to hold on to their human tenderness and sensitivity.

A fawn is an extremely delicate and slender being that has lost almost all its animal wildness. It is also a ruminant. If we transfer these physical characteristics to the spiritual we see a depiction of a human being, delicate and a bit bestial, but thank goodness also a ruminant! If humans were not ruminants in the spiritual sense, how could they ever develop higher skills?

The deeply saddened, loyal sister now slips her garter over the fawn's head, makes a lead from bulrush and leads the little animal through the forest. We can now reiterate what we said above: the soul that is (unconsciously) led by the higher I leads the fallen lower I.

They finally find an empty little house in the forest. There they settle and Little Sister cares lovingly for the fawn; mankind slowly begins to feel at home (finds his home) in the darkness of earthly life and continues to work on his task: to lead his lower I with all its desires.

Then something very strange happens that will surprise many of us. Nevertheless, it is one of the most wonderful fairy tale images imaginable: the king's hunting party passes through the forest. The horns sound and the fawn, hearing the horns, jumps up. He wants to be hunted by the king! Little Sister is worried and tries to hold him back, just as she did at the springs: "You may get hurt or even killed!" But the little fawn cannot be held back and scampers into the forest.

We must now leave every logical thought behind. We must now silence our everyday reasoning and keep from saying something like "the fawn didn't know what danger awaited him and wanted to have a look" in order to conceal the apparent incongruity of what is happening here. On the contrary. We should emphasize what this is all about. Through its outward inexplicability, the inner truth of the image will speak that much more strongly to the child's soul: the fawn heard the king's horns sound. It could not be stopped; it had to be hunted by the king! His little sister had to let him go. The little thing runs outside and is immediately followed by the hunters, throughout the day.

Why does the little fawn so desperately want to be hunted by the king? Why does it run outside knowing that it might find death out there?

The key to this question is the king.

The lower I, stuck in its desires (the fawn), is led through life by the soul (the sister). But the soul cannot free the lower I. This can only be done by the higher I when inspired by the spirit. The higher I almost never intervenes openly in daily life, but sometimes we get a flash: our "king" (our I) announces itself like the king's hunting horns. The higher I comes to test the lower I in order to free it from its bonds; it comes to "hunt" the lower I! If the lower I is still early in its development, then it won't want to be "hunted" by the higher I: it will avoid the hunt. But if it is further along and perhaps ready to be freed, it will want nothing more than to be tested (hunted) by the spirit that works through the higher I so that it can finally become a true human being. It can even happen that the lower I recognizes the test, in other words, starts to understand the path of development, and longs for the tests to begin so that it can be freed. It longs "to be hunted by the king." The soul that has led the lower I until now must obey the inspiration coming from the higher I. Little Sister must give in to the call of the horns: she must let the fawn go.

All things considered, every person's task is to allow ourselves to be "hunted" by our "king" (our higher I). If a person comes to this point and has developed a certain level of consciousness, he will usually be able to hear his "king's horn" in the distance as destiny sends a task his way. Instead of complaining, he will come out of his home, just like the fawn, and give himself fully to being "hunted" by his "king," freeing him from his "enchantment."

Our soul heard the horn of the king who wanted to hunt us long before birth, in the worldly midnight hour of our pre-birth, the moment when our soul had to find a new earthly existence. The nourishing time in heaven had to be exchanged for the dark, painful, earthly life needed for further development. The soul hears the mighty horns and allows itself to be called into the darkness by its spirit-king. It must work to conquer the darkness by finding *new* light and letting it shine.

These great pre-birth events repeat themselves in life after birth in all kinds of variations both large and small. For example, a boy who is about thirteen or fourteen years old is obsessed with doing dangerous things. His parents will reprimand him repeatedly, just as the little sister tried to keep the fawn at home in the fairy tale. The parents are often right but it is very important that they understand that their son has reached an age when the soul hears the I's "horn." The horn calls the boy to go through tests that must open his consciousness for the "king" (the I) so that he can become an *individual.*

This does not mean that the higher I will now enter the boy! However, the horn has sounded and the hunting party comes closer.

These are life processes that every healthy boy and girl goes through during pre-adolescence and adolescence. In girls the process is more disguised. Destiny sounds the horn for the I of adults and sets them before the necessary tests. It is then up to them and their development to hear the sound and follow it or to let themselves be kept at home by their worried "sister" who has always been there for them and has led them so lovingly through life but who cannot recognize the approaching "king I."

Literature gives us many examples of people who let themselves be "hunted" by the I. Every legend is an example. In the Old Testament, Jacob fights with the angel. In this story, the "hunt" is portrayed as a fight between Jacob and his higher I, in which the spiritual world lives and speaks. When dawn breaks, the angel wants to leave but Jacob, feeling that the fight was not enough, says to the angel: "I won't let you go unless you bless me!" The angel blesses Jacob, meaning Jacob receives a higher initiation in the spirit than he previously had, allowing him to become a patriarch. From then on, he was called "Israel," Fighter for God.

This story shows us the positive side to "being hunted" or "fighting with" the higher I and the spiritual world. It tells us not to avoid these trials but to face them courageously. But the fight can also be dangerous, as when Jacob's hip is injured.

In the fairy tale, the fawn comes closer to being freed from its enchantment, in other words to becoming human again, but it is injured during the hunt. The hunting party, following the trail of blood (the marks of a struggle), arrives at the little house. Thus, the king finds the little sister (the I reaches the soul) and wants to take her with him to his castle: the spiritual world. The soul is allowed to be initiated: but she remains faithful to the lower I (the fawn). "It must come too," she says. In other words, humanity that stands before the initiation into the spiritual world says: "the lower part of my being must also be purified. Otherwise the initiation is not true, it is only a disguise."

The king agrees and takes the girl onto his horse, a wonderful image that we see in many fairy tales: the I that moves in the spirit (on a fast, high horse) takes the soul, which previously walked the earth on foot, with him and lets her partake in his uplifted, quick pace.

The Little Sister and the fawn come to live with the king. The wedding (initiation) takes place. The soul and the lower I have entered the realm of the higher I and will now be governed by the higher I, even though the lower I is still an animal. Mankind, which has reached a certain level of initiation, will not necessarily have conquered all his weaknesses and faults. It is possible to attain a high level of development in some respects while staying seriously behind in others. Thus, when reaching an ever-higher level of initiation, progressively more dangerous tests present themselves, and the soul can fall that much harder if it fails a test.

In most fairy tales these later, more dangerous tests are not depicted. The initiation in the spirit is presented as a single, definitive event. Once the wedding between the girl and the prince or the king has taken place, the couple lives happily ever after and the story ends.

But in "Little Brother and Little Sister," serious challenges present themselves after Little Sister marries the king and becomes queen.

The stepmother hears that her stepchildren are doing very well, and is furious. On top of that, her own ugly, one-eyed daughter wants to become queen instead of the little sister. In other words, "stepmother Earth" (spiritually deprived earthly life) does not grant a good life to people who develop spiritually. Her "own daughter" (the materialistic human soul that is only interested in the outside) is jealous and says: "the power over earthly life is *mine* because I am Mother Earth's 'own' child!" "OK," says Mother Earth to the spiritually ugly one-eyed people who only see the world from one side, "I will make you queen!"[2]

In the meantime, a prince is born in the castle: the soul (the queen), led by the I, can create new (spiritual) life on earth. In the language of fairy tales, she has given life to a little prince. We have already discussed that delivering a child cannot be understood by children as the work of the mother and as such should not be brought to the consciousness of young children. However, in fairy tales bringing new life can work well as an *image* of creation.

But the king is not at home for the birth—he is hunting. In other words, the I is not alert: it has not thought about the traps and deceptions that lurk around every new creation. It does not protect the soul. Therefore the "opposing powers," the stepmother and her daughter, can act. They take the queen's life (temporarily) and replace her with the one-eyed daughter. This also happens in us, of course: if our I is not watchful, purity and innocence are exchanged for deceit and selfishness, even if we want to develop our soul to a higher level.

Another character now joins the story: the wet nurse who guards the cradle. If darkness secretly takes over our being and even the I does not detect it, there is always something in the soul that stays watchful and objective through all the deceit. This is the only thing that can see through or feel all falsehoods. This is the part of our soul that stays connected to the child powers and that continues to guard our innocence (the "child in us"). She is the "wet nurse" in our being: our good instincts. It is this part that feels that the real queen has been replaced by another being. The "wet nurse" protects the "child" in us who has lost his mother.

We now see a very fine web between the conscious and dream worlds. Few fairy tales have such a masterfully created, extremely fine web.

The wet nurse, who has a dreamy consciousness, has a vision of the mother during the night. She does not speak at first but the nurse sees that she lovingly strokes a child and a fawn. The nurse sees this vision a number of times. Finally, the nurse hears the vision speak, and she tells the king everything she has seen and heard. He now comes to guard as well: the I has been warned by the instinctive feelings and observations of the soul (by the nurse) and finally awakens. The king's higher consciousness allows him to immediately understand what the spirit of the queen is saying. She is asking after her child (their mutual "creation") and the fawn (the lower I that she was supposed to take care of).

The king listens quietly. Unlike our lower being, which wants to react to everything immediately, our higher I can hold back: it can be silent, and silently listen. It quietly internalizes everything deep into its consciousness.

When the event is experienced a second time by the king the next night, he also hears the vision say: "I will not return anymore." This time, he rises, walks towards her and embraces her saying: "You are no one other than my true queen!"

The enchantment has now been broken! Because the king has spoken to and recognized her, the queen returns to life: if our I consciousness recognizes and speaks to the lost soul in its true form then it can find its way back and reign over life as a queen together with the king (the I). The soul has reached an even higher consciousness, which can finally conquer evil.

The king now lets the courts judge the evil stepmother and the one-eyed daughter. The one-eyed daughter is brought into the forest, where she is eaten by wild beasts. This is the destiny of the one-eyed, atavistic, egotistically persistent part of our soul. In the end it is consumed by beastly lust. The stepmother is burned, just like the weeds that are picked out of the wheat harvest, tied in bundles and burned (Matthew 12:24-30). At the end of this dramatic story, the witch from the beginning of the tale is tried and thrown into the fire. The flames of the spirit consume her.

Once the witch has turned into ashes, the enchantment over the brother breaks: the fawn once again becomes a human child and Little Brother and Little Sister are reunited. They now live together with the king. Once persistent evil in us (the witch), which also causes extreme one-sidedness, can no longer develop because it has been burned by the spiritual fire, our beastly side is changed and we can become true human beings again. Then our soul and our now refined lower I can live together with our higher I, our "king."

In a very new and different way, this fairy tale also gives us an image of how humanity can follow its great path of development.

---

**ENDNOTES**

1 For further discussion of young children and "amphibiousness," see Udo de Haes, *The Singing, Playing Kindergarten*, Chapter 7.

2 In many fairy tales and myths, having only one eye indicates clairvoyant abilities (Cyclops in Greek mythology; Odin who can see everything with his one eye; giants in many fairy tales). In this fairy tale, it suggests an atavistic soul connection that cannot find the right way to earthly life and turns to ever-stronger materialistic and demonic excesses.

# 5 | How to choose and tell fairy tales

## "Life fairy tales"

The development of mankind can be seen as one large happening. Each human life reflects this development in its own way, by following its own destiny, its own path in the extensive fabric of this phenomenon.

The fairy tales reflect this development in their own language of images. Each fairy tale has its own specific character, language, and motifs.

If we put these two together, it will not surprise us that every child has a favorite fairy tale. Often a child will want to hear one particular tale over and over again. This is what we can call a "life fairy tale," the tale with which a child grows up.

The question that immediately arises is: is this okay? Is it not too one-sided? Should we be led by this desire to hear one tale over and over again?

First of all, repeating one fairy tale does not mean that we tell this fairy tale exclusively. We can tell many tales but then always come back to that one, favorite story.

Why is this so important?

In ancient times, when medicine was made from herbs, it was

often said that no disease existed that could not be cured by an herb. This was not an exaggeration or fantasy. Today, these relationships have changed. Humanity prefers synthetic chemical medicines and has therefore lost touch with the herbs, which are not as harsh. However, this old truth still exists. Not only does mankind have a relationship with the animal kingdom, as discussed in "The Donkey," it also has a relationship with plants. Plants have a particular connection with our physical growth and building up of strength. Each human organ, each function of the human body can be seen in the character and life of a certain type of plant. Conversely, every tree, every herb has a relationship with certain life processes in parts of the human body. Thus, when an organ cannot function as it should, there is a specific herb whose sap and tissue can help the healing process.

This connection between the physical and etheric realms can also be seen in the light of the soul world of early childhood and the world of fairy tales. If we change the wording slightly, we could say that each healthy interest or healthy development of a child's soul has a complementary fairy tale that will give special nourishment.

Healthy children have many interests; they have an abundance of impulses. Music, melodies, and rhythms often have a certain "theme" or "leitmotif." Similarly, that which lives in a child's soul is usually imbued with one principle that dominates her development. The child will therefore long for the fairy tale that gives her what *she* needs for her development. This particular fairy tale is "nourishment" for her soul.

Thus, it is important to ascertain which fairy tale is the "life fairy tale" of each child in our care. We can then alternate the various tales and, of course, add other ones. Besides giving the children a precious gift for life, we will also be able to take a deeper look into their essence by finding out which fairy tale is *their* fairy tale. It should be obvious that we should only respond to healthy interests of the children. A fairy tale about cars or a robot can only be damaging and will not encourage healthy development.

We cannot draw any conclusions as to which child will want to hear which fairy tale. However, it will be obvious that a child more interested in the shrewd, brave little tailor wants a completely different "herb" for his soul than the child who repeatedly asks to hear about poor Cinderella, who has to stay at home. It is important that these interests are seen in their relationship with each child's other qualities. Only then must they be allowed to speak to us and can we come to a conclusion. Additionally, it should be obvious that the developmental possibilities that we mean to see are also connected with the character and the temperament of each child. We will now discuss the four temperaments in relation to the above in the next part of this chapter[1].

## Fairy tales and the temperaments

Parents and caregivers can consider the temperaments when choosing which fairy tale to tell to certain children. Admittedly, temperaments usually do not become clear until after the seventh year, but they can begin to play an active role in many children earlier in life. It can therefore be good to pay attention to this in the telling of fairy tales.

Choleric children are most open to tales that express actions, strength and courage; melancholic children prefer sad tales; sanguines prefer tales that have quick changes, and phlegmatics prefer peaceful, and languid tales. In short, every child craves fairy tales that fit his temperament.

But doesn't a fairy tale that expresses the same temperament of the child exaggerate that temperament, increasing its domination of the child?

No. The "herbs" of the world of fairy tales work

"homeopathically" on the child's temperament. If we were to tell a sanguine fairy tale, with all its quick changes, to a phlegmatic child, it would not hit home and the child would not "hear" it. He would sink even further into his phlegmatic nature and even into apathy. The phlegmatic feels at home in a calm, elaborate tale: he can internalize the contents and possibly arrive at such a level of joy and liveliness, that his phlegmatic nature is largely conquered. A melancholic fairy tale works similarly on the melancholic child: the sad fate of a poor girl who eventually marries the prince and becomes queen comforts the child and makes her feel understood. A sanguine child calms down when hearing a tale that jumps from here to there, because the tale satisfies his need for activity. The choleric child is satisfied by a tale that tells of powerful deeds. Otherwise she may feel the need to express her desire for intense acts in her surroundings. The hero of the story performs the deeds that the child feels in her bones; the child's soul actively participates, and thus feels content.

We therefore observe that fairy tales that correspond with temperaments are good for children. If there are a number of children in the group, at school, in the kindergarten, or at home, it is good to divide the children into four groups and give each group its turn: that is, give each group its needed nourishment and satisfaction. Obviously, the children with different temperaments will hear the fairy tale meant for someone else. They might have more difficulty with it, but it will also nourish them in a different way. Didactically and socially it will be good if we tell the group a tale that has been chosen for a group, or maybe even for one specific child. In the end, when all the temperaments have had their turn, we will have silently encouraged social engagement as well.

## How do we tell different fairy tales for specific temperaments?

The way we tell fairy tales can promote healthy integration of the four temperaments. We have already discussed narration style in general. To this we can add that the homeopathic principle is most effective if we tell the fairy tale without exaggeration, and let the tale speak for itself. We should tell a melancholic tale melancholically, a choleric tale cholerically, and so forth. A phlegmatic tale needs to be told calmly, a sanguine tale needs liveliness in its narration. If we use these suggestions, the workings of the fairy tale will be that much stronger.

Some fairy tales represent more than one temperament; these we can make fit a particular temperament in our style of narration. "The Brave Little Tailor" can be told for a sanguine child (seven birds with one stone!), and also for a choleric child if we emphasize the tailor's courage. "The Frog Prince" can express the phlegmatic *and* sanguine nature of the frog, and later the choleric actions of the princess. In "Little Brother and Little Sister," the melancholic element is obvious but the choleric/sanguine aspect of the fawn can also play a part.

But remember that emotions and moods should never be portrayed naturalistically. However enraged the king becomes, his rage is a "fairy tale rage," expressed with a dark tone of voice and a furrowed brow. Grief, even for the death of a loved one, must remains an illustrated, "fairy tale" grief. The child *sees* the grief of the prince or princess and is carried away with it in his fairy tale fantasy world, but he does not experience it as being real. This is important because it will help him remain in the image world needed for his development.

Thus, the moods and emotions as well as the content of the fairy tales have a suprapersonal image character, meaning that one should remain calm *inside* no matter what temperament the fairy tale expresses. Quick changes can be expressed while remaining calm on the inside; carefully choosing words and not tripping over them will preserve the effect of the tale. A quiet *ground tone* is needed no matter what swings of temperament or mood the fairy tale contains.

## How many fairy tales is enough?

When we observe the intense effect a fairy tale has on a child, and how deeply and joyfully its contents are internalized, we instinctively know not to be too generous in the number of tales we tell. An overabundance can easily be avoided even when working with a large group of children, such as a class or playgroup. In the end, there are only *four* temperaments, and each can have its turn. It is especially important to limit the number of fairy tales told for very young children (three- and four-year-olds). After all, every fairy tale has a long way to go to be completely internalized by the essence of the child. In this case, it is best to select only a few tales and return to them again and again. If a "life fairy tale" has been detected, it can be told more often, according to the wishes of the children. Healthy children will want to hear the tales to which they feel a connection again and again.

For older children (five, six, or seven years of age), the number of tales can be expanded. However, one should never tell more than one fairy tale per day. If we do tell more than one, the effect of the one will disturb the effect of the other during the night and neither will be able to enter the child's soul.

If we take all these things into account, we will be able to decide easily which and how many tales can be told in various circumstances.

## The craving for "new" and "true" stories

As mentioned above, healthy children will not repeatedly ask for new fairy tales. On the contrary. They will long for the familiar tale again and again—the importance of which we need not repeat.

However, children whose development is not healthy are different. For example, let's take a precocious child who has never really heard a fairy tale and has seen only had simple picture books from the local corner store: energetically drawn, "fun," but free of content and without nourishment for the child's soul. How can such a child, once a kindergartner, ask for anything other than exciting new stories?

The old fairy tales do nothing for him. He is not interested in the content, is not attracted to the nourishment that fairy tales give the child's soul; he only wants to satisfy his thirst for never-ending stimulation. The spiritual world is for him so far away, so completely hidden by the external world, that a "recollection," created by fairy tales in healthy children, is hardly possible anymore.

No wonder most of these children want to hear "true" stories, or stories that could be "true." People who lack a connection with the images expressed in fairy tales are often inclined to a life of external impulses. They think that these tendencies in their children show a healthy dose of reality. They are not aware that this preference for externality is not a healthy preference for reality, but an impoverishment through the loss of something that should still be a reality: the spiritual world in which the child should still be living.

If we allow the child's outward interests to prevail, then we cause the world that should have been the foundation for the rest of his life to close for him completely and forever. The young child is then banished from *his* paradise, just as Adam and Eve were banished, while he only understands little useless aspects of the new, externally oriented world in which he has been put before his time: child*like* becomes child*ish*.

Furthermore, children who are prematurely subjected to the external world, having learned to understand it in a childish way, have grave difficulties ridding themselves of this understanding. Changing this banal way of looking at things learned at a very early age results in narrow-mindedness. Only those of us who have been allowed to open our hearts to the spiritual images of fairy tales as small children will be able to learn to understand the true greatness of the spiritual image language of life and of the world as adults.

To summarize, the development of the child is not improved, and may even be seriously damaged, if we continually tell new stories, especially if these tales only speak about external life or "actual" events.

Of course, a child who is accustomed to these real stories cannot suddenly be cut off from them. If we did this, she would find the old fairy tales even more boring and resent them. However, it is possible to lead her back to the right path of development step by step. We must guide her back to the lost land of childhood tactfully and lovingly.

This is not easy. It asks for much patience and many of us will give up after a number of tries. If we remember that this is about rediscovering or recreating the foundations for the rest of the child's life no effort will be too much, no sacrifice too great.

But how do we do this? We have to look at the circumstances and at the child. And of course each of us has our own capabilities. Let's look at an example.

At the end of the day, after all the hubbub and stimulation that the child has experienced and internalized during the day, we take the child to bed and spend time alone with her. We try to create a cozy and warm atmosphere. In the beginning, the child will not tolerate this warm, quiet coziness. She jumps up, runs about, and doesn't listen. Don't pay attention to this behavior. Just continue quietly telling a really beautiful fairy tale. But spend only a *very short* time. In the beginning only five minutes, or even less. When you are finished, the child will sigh with relief: the torment has passed.

However, the next day, the "torture" is repeated. The fairy tale is continued, not compulsively but with a friendly determination, every day, again and again. Then one day, having almost forgotten the ritual and even though she has only cursed it until now, you are reminded of it by the child: "Aren't you going to tell the story tonight?" You realize that the beginning of the story, which seemed to have passed the child by completely, has been internalized: ". . . but the father loved the children. Why did he leave them in the forest?" And there will be more questions that look back on what was previously told. Thus, the quiet and coziness allows the child's heart to thaw slowly. True childhood is starting to unfold in her soul.

It is best not to tell the chosen story in one sitting. Leave the next part to the next day, spreading the story out over a number of days. This will give the child a certain amount of tension, something that she is so used to and cannot do without yet. Later on this can be done differently.

Our biggest ally in the healing process is the night. During the night, the fairy tale works on, unhindered by the child's objections. It is important to develop a consciousness for this effect.

After a few days or weeks, try to take fifteen or thirty minutes during the day—if needed together with the child—to let her try and draw a picture of the fairy tale. Healthy children are left to do this on their own: they draw from their experiences, from their imagination, something we adults can no longer do. If the adult is also drawing, the young child, always eager to imitate, will undoubtedly be influenced by our more externally focused way of drawing. This will be detrimental to his own imaginative capabilities. It will be very difficult for a nervous, intellectually oriented child, who has slid into external experiences, to express himself in drawing. If you let him join the rest of the children in a playgroup, he will eventually loosen up. If he is alone, drawing with him as a transition will inevitably be needed. We can only hope that a part of the lost imaginative qualities will return once he has been able to draw by himself. It is not necessary to be able to draw when accompanying a child. The most important thing is that quiet, peace, and dedication are given to the child in a friendly manner, during which the fairy tale and what it tries to portray are contemplated in more depth.[2]

If the above advice is followed and difficulties are not avoided by giving up, the much-needed lost connection with fairy tales and the world of the child in general can be recovered. It is most important that you keep at it, slowly, quietly, and with utmost patience and love.

If the child is too old for fairy tales, consider *The Wonderful Adventures of Nils* by Selma Lagerlöf, or *Pinocchio*, or any other age-appropriate book.

As we have already said, a different path will have to be found and followed for every child. Whichever path is followed, something of what has been lost but still lies deeply concealed within the child will be brought to new life (see also "Children who reject fairy tales").

All of the above takes much time and quiet, something that we do not have a lot of in our modern world. The more time people save by using modern technology, the less time they have to spend, even with their children. This punishes us because more and more children ask for extra time and quiet. The only possibility is that we make time and quiet and that we give this newly found time to our children with love.

## For the youngest children: what about happy endings?

We have already said that it is better not to tell too many different fairy tales to the youngest children. The younger the child, the deeper the experience and effect of the fairy tale. Thus, it is the youngest children that we rob of inner peace if we tell too many tales. The images will compete with each other.

For the same reason, it is important to choose short and simple fairy tales for the youngest children. A good example is the tale about the child whose friend was a toad. The child's mother found this friendship disgusting and killed the toad, and then the child withered away and died. This is a short rendition of the story. It will, however, be important to change the ending into something positive, as in "Mother Holle." For example, the child does not die but digs a grave for the poor toad and comes to visit him every day. She becomes increasingly unhappy and remains so overwhelmed with grief that her mother is afraid she will die. But then one day, when the girl is at the grave and her tear drops on the earth, the earth opens and the toad rises from the dead, no longer a toad but a beautiful prince. They marry and live happily ever after.

The difficult words that some of the fairy tales use should not be avoided. Although the youngest child will not know the literal *meaning* of the words, she is deeply susceptible to the tone mystery. Therefore, be careful not to give explanations that are only directed at intellectual understanding, as they can disrupt the experience of the words mystery. Understanding will come later (see "Sounds carry the content").

A positive ending can also correspond with reality. One could say that if the soul must lose its connection with the pre-birth world after the kindergarten phase, especially around adolescence and represented by the bestial (the toad) that can live in its "pre-birth element," water, the soul does not die completely but withers away. The spiritual world in its old form has died for her: the toad is dead and thus the soul pines away. However, if she remains true to her old friend, he can rise again in a completely new form.

We would also like to express the sincere wish that the change of ending that we have suggested for the fairy tale above will actually take place in the world of early childhood. Doesn't this small child live in two worlds at the same time (earth *and* the pre-birth spiritual world)? Isn't this natural "amphibiousness" being threatened, if not extinguished, by our modern way of living?[3] The "toad," the "amphibian" *within* the young child is being killed, resulting in the loss of the *true nature* of early childhood. Let us hope that more insight into the true essence of the young child will stop this fatal development and that it will be transformed into an advantageous ending.

But why should a happy ending be preferable?

First of all, negative or unhappy endings make the child feel helpless within. This effect is burdensome to his development and could even affect the formation of his organs. A happy ending has a corresponding, positive effect on his entire being.

The following should also be added. Young children carry a deep connection with the development of mankind as a whole from their pre-birth existence. This is why most fairy tales express the entire development of mankind, or the complete development of the world through to a luminous ending as one all-inclusive whole. This helps the young child to rediscover the totality of the world that she still carries within, in the earthly world. Thus, her soul can say "yes" to fairy tales and to earthly life.

As we know, young children search within for the totality of things. If a fairy tale does not speak of the complete development of mankind and ends on an unfavorable note, this says to the young child, "everything is going wrong for the world!" Think how destructive this would be for the child's development. Even we adults could not bear such an ending. How could the divine world leader have begun creation and let the Fall of Mankind take place if there was not light at the end of the tunnel? The entire world would then become pointless. The same is true for the young child who still lives partly in the spiritual world. Getting stuck in the darkness completely robs creation of its meaning. If we give a young child a dark ending, then we weaken part of her foundations for the rest of her life.

So we should not hesitate to give fairy tales a positive ending for the youngest children, even if it means changing the original version. Just make sure that the new ending has meaning and is created tastefully.

Let's return to our initial question: Which fairy tales do we choose for the youngest children? The fairy tale should be short and simple, with great meaning, and intellectual understanding should not yet play a part. A fairy tale such as "Puss in Boots," in which the cat's calculated tricks strongly appeal to thinking, is not recommended for the youngest children. For the small ones, tricks in general should be avoided, and fairy tales should appeal more to the will than to thinking. However, one should not think that the character of the fairy tale should be elementary and plain—on the contrary. The images should be so grand in their simplicity, so truthful in what they are saying, that they affect the deepest parts of the soul, in which the will finds its origins. "The Wolf and the Seven Young Goats" is a perfect example.

Many other short, simple fairy tales by the Brothers Grimm are good for the three- and four-year-olds in your group.

## Fairy tales for older children

Older children will find longer and more intricate fairy tales more interesting. They do not get lost as easily when a story is more elaborate. Now we can choose long fairy tales such as "The Two Brothers," "The Water of Life," "Faithful John," etc. (all from the Brothers Grimm). These tales are too difficult for the youngest children. Thinking and understanding as well as more subjective feeling start playing an important role.

Together with the element of thought, tricks and skill become more important. We all know how much children at the age of five or six love small heroes such as Tom Thumb, who conquers a dull giant using his firmness and alertness. These children have arrived at an age where the intellect, personified in a small "clever hero" (sometimes a "little rascal") must yield to the concealed physical forces (the "dumb giant") by which they have been led dreamily until now. They are going through a transition period, just as mankind in general did many centuries ago. Thought begins to take the lead over instincts and other natural impulses.

A perfect image of the awakening intellect is "The Brave Little Tailor" with his sharp needle (Grimm) who is too clever for everyone and even outsmarts the "giants" (the forces of nature) in the forest. Children in this transition phase always adore this fairy tale.

It is also good to give them this nourishment now. A specific quality must be developed in each phase of life and each should be supported during its development. Thus, when the children are five and six, *thinking* (on a childlike level, of course) and everything that has to do with thinking, such as cleverness and quick-wittedness, should be encouraged.

Other virtues, such as courage, patience, loyalty, and love, now all include some thinking. Thinking becomes a part of every life function. All emotional life and all actions start to become more conscious. Even humor becomes different. Humor was important for the youngest children, but it did not yet include understanding. It was therefore "cuter." Now humor becomes "funny." "Clever Grethel," mentioned earlier in this book, or "Puss in Boots" are both full of clever tricks and humor, despite the contrasts in their characterizations. Both fairy tales even commend cleverness above truth, something that we also spoke about earlier and that is completely justified at this age (see "About morals in fairy tales and fables").

This brings us to Hans Christian Andersen, whose ironic, sometimes even sarcastic humor can be so subtle that it often does not become conscious until adulthood. Andersen is also often very elaborate, making him one of the great storytellers. However, most important is that he tells us great truths. The brilliant fairy tale moods that he creates equal those of the ancient fairy tales, a feat not easily achieved.

Thus, we have come to an area in which we can work from an adult awareness, moreso than with the youngest children. However, we must never forget that the developmental difference between the children and us is still quite large.

All in all, we should now have a number of different possibilities from which we can make a right choice with regards to which fairy tale to tell which age group.

## Preparing to tell fairy tales

Anyone who has experience telling fairy tales knows that telling is actually recreating them, especially if we keep various factors, such as the temperaments in our audience, in mind. We must be able to create freely. Of course, this is only possible if we know the fairy tale through and through and don't *read* it but *tell* it. This is extremely difficult for people in our time as nobody seems to have, or permits themselves to have, enough time to prepare.

If you really do not have time, reading a fairy tale is better than nothing. Reading can be very lively and worth a lot, but the only way to reach children in each of their special qualities and let the fairy tale be fully appreciated is to tell the story. For one, you are completely free in choosing the tone, words, movements, everything about the way the contents are interpreted. The fairy tale can be reborn, something that can only happen through the teller.

Furthermore, by working with the fairy tale with deep respect but with free and new creative energy, one forms a close and intimate connection with it, which is a prerequisite for a lively and effective rendition. This is best achieved if enough time is taken for the preparation, preferably a number of days.

There is another, deeper reason. It may sound strange or it may seem obvious, but we do not want to leave it unmentioned. When we fall asleep at night, we leave our day consciousness behind. Our "I" and part of our soul retreat from our body. Of course, they do not disappear; they "pass over" to the world of the spirit, their home. However, the important inner living tasks that they confronted themselves with during the day, including internalizing and trying to formulate a fairy tale, remain essential in the spiritual world. In this world, the tasks "grow" and become clearer; not to the effect that all problems are solved, but that they are enriched and broadened by the spiritual powers that help us. We become connected with the deepest essence of the task: we are completely imbued by it, even if it does not occur in our dreams. When we awake, our view of the task is much broader than it was yesterday. It has a new and much grander character. We might be surprised because we have no idea where this has come from. These are the gifts that are given to us by the spirits during the night.

If we learn to understand the language of the spirit, we will experience the same thing as the "diligent girl" in the fairy tale "Mother Holle." Our soul, so diligent during the day (in this case with preparing the fairy tale), comes into the spiritual realm of

"Mother Holle" during the night. There, our soul is filled with the work it has done during the day and what it still wants to achieve. Mother Holle blesses this work and lets a golden rain fall on the soul. This gold stays with us, and the next day its radiance falls on everyone to whom our work is dedicated.

Spiritual help during the night and nightly inspiration takes place for our every undertaking. It is possible to learn to open one's soul organs to these powers.

The snow, like in "Mother Holle," can show us what we can achieve through our diligent preparations. During the night, we visit the source of the "snowflakes": the good ideas and impulses that come down from the spiritual world to mankind. The next day, when we sit across from the children to tell them the fairy tale, it could very well be that it continually "snows" as the tale is told: endless good ideas, perfect words, telling gestures and facial expressions come forth for the children toabsorb. We can thank "Mother Holle" for this, or actually the spiritual forces that we met during the night as we carried our task to them.

We will not get this spiritual help if we don't use at least one night for preparation. However, it is even worse if you have not prepared at all and just "jump in."

Be it as it may, there will be circumstances in which preparation is impossible. We can then only repeat what we have said before: telling the story unprepared is better than not telling the story at all.

## Sounds carry the content

There is something unusual that we witness time and time again when telling a fairy tale to children. They want the tale to be told with exactly the same words each time. If we have used the word "chops" for the wolf once, we cannot change it to "mouth." If we do use the new word, we will be corrected immediately.

Witnessing this is funny, but we must understand that it is also important. It shows us how close these children still are to the origins of words.

Adults without an excessively poetic nature hear the *meaning* of words instead of the sounds from which they originate. This is why "chops" and a "mouth" are almost the same for us. For children, especially the youngest, they are completely different. When they first hear the word "chops" in the fairy tale, the word has no meaning but is a collection of sounds; it is a "tone mystery." Within this tone mystery, for which the children get a sense through the tale, lies the concealed crux of what brings the tale home. How could we possibly say a completely different word built up of completely different sounds?

Since this strong connection to the world of sounds, which is much more intense than that of meaning, is healthy and normal for this age group and beneficial to the development of the child, we should keep to certain words and sounds for certain fairy tales. These sounds are what carry the content of the tale.

## Refrain from explaining the stories

Something else that may be obvious is that we should never disclose anything regarding the background or hidden meaning of fairy tales to the children. For one, they are not open to such explanations (see "Why metaphors and not concepts?"). Young children will not understand. If we try to explain the tale, it will be detrimental to them, as their thinking consciousness would be awakened prematurely. They would lose a good deal of their image experience as well as much of their imagination, which would in turn affect their development in general. It is just as important for the adult to know about the backgrounds and the essence of the fairy tales as it is for the children not to know. Thus, this book, that only speaks about early childhood and fairy tales, is a book for adults and certainly not for children. Take care not to tell the children anything about the contents of this book. These contents can only be valuable to the young child if they lead to ideas, ideals, and actions *coming from the reader in relationship to the young child.*

## Refrain from preaching

Many people are tempted to use fairy tales as moral lessons. For example, in "Mary's Child" (Jacob Grimm), the forbidden thirteenth gate is opened but the girl denies having opened it. Her punishment is that she has to leave her home in the heavens. We could easily follow this tale and with a wagging finger, saying: "See what happens when you aren't honest?" If we do this, we forget that fairy tale dishonesty is on a completely different plane from that of our daily life. Behind each gate, the girl found an apostle, and behind the thirteenth gate she found the Trinity, which she had not previously seen. We can also see this as another image of eating the forbidden fruit, after which we had to leave paradise. The fairy tale is completely reduced if we bring it to an everyday level, not as an image but as an outer reality, especially if every little offense is part of the greater human drama. If a child connects opening the thirteenth heavenly gate with telling little white lies, he could lose the possibility of experiencing this immense event in its true dimensions later in life.

We have already said that a fairy tale's moral extends far beyond daily life. Therefore, it offers wonderful possibilities for the future, for the child as well as for all humanity. This possibility is lost if fairy tales are used as "Moraalsäure" (moral acid, an expression used in the Rudolf Steiner School in Stuttgart).

## Choosing illustrated fairy tales

Are illustrations are needed for fairy tales? That is a good question. If we take time and become still, creating the right atmosphere to tell a fairy tale, the most wonderful and lively images will arise in the child's soul by themselves. These images allow her to relive the still depths of her pre-birth world. However, a dreamy experience of her spiritual origins can arise not only by hearing, but also by seeing. The experience thereby becomes that much more vivid, creating immeasurable value for the rest of her life.

But there are prerequisites. An illustration must exude the same feeling that the teller is trying to create, as well as the spiritual origins that are created by the tale itself.

I personally remember the intense experiences given to me as a child by illustrations to "Tom Thumb" and "Little Red Riding Hood" by Gustave Doré. Ludwig Richter, Arthur Rackham, and Edmund Dulac also have much to offer.

Today, we have to be very careful in choosing illustrations. There are many wonderful illustrators, but where is the fairy tale mood? We have to search for it, like a needle in a haystack. Anton Pieck, for example, skillfully illustrates what a romantic adult experiences when listening to fairy tales, but he does not access the secret world of early childhood. Then there are the "nice pictures" by Rie Cramer that illustrate her poems about childhood. Both hide emptiness behind their cute depictions of "sweet everyday life" and belie the higher origins of the child. Finally, we have the "funny," well-drawn modern fairy tale illustrations. Walt Disney shows us fairy tale kings (that should represent high, even spiritual worlds for the child) and little gnomes that represent mischievous jokesters with red drunkard's noses; princes, princesses, and other heroes with grotesquely distorted eyes, and animals with clown-like sneers. In these expensive books (let's not even talk about the cheap ones), we find fairy tales that try to tell us about the higher pre-birth world in a honky-tonk way.

Thank goodness there are fairy tale illustrators who do not follow this path. Some, like Rie Reindersma, also take the tales seriously. However, I do not know of a modern illustrator who fully opens the world of fairy tales to us.

Another art form that could tempt us is abstract or non-figurative art. This art can be very important for adults as the figurative sense-world experience is not triggered when only color, light and dark, form, line and proportions are seen. However, this kind of artwork does not belong in the fairy tale experience of early childhood. The young child is in a transitional phase from the non-figurative, spiritual world to the figurative earthly world. It is his "task" to recognize the living spirit in earthly objects. Fairy tales help him with this task. They describe the spirit and the development of the spirit figuratively in characters and actions, and guide the young child into our figurative world. Abstract or non-figurative art undoes the sense world's form and appearance, something that should be the guiding light for the young child. How can he possibly find his way without this guidance? Nevertheless, young children are open to direct color and form experiences, but not when it is meant as an illustration for a figurative image.

Another interesting creation is the book with foldout pages in which certain cutout figures jump out, creating a three-dimensional effect. This creates a realistic level of perspective that we adults like very much. How does the young child see this?

Flat pictures that awaken the still-present imaginative connection with the spiritual world now jump out: the dreamy spiritual experience is changed into an outer sense experience. The young child is alienated from his spiritual origins and restricted by outer experiences. He is torn out of his childhood dream and thrown into the "cold world" just like the cutout figure in the book. He is forced to take a step that he should not have to take until he is older. This seemingly small step can seriously deprive him in his development.

It is understandable that illustrators do not feel as bound by tradition as those who tell fairy tales. This gives us an extra reason to be careful when showing young children illustrated fairy tales. Let's hope that new connections with the fairy tale world will soon be made in the art of illustration.

## Dare to make mistakes

Those who did not grow up with fairy tales might feel overwhelmed by all the advice contained in this book. If you feel this way, please just let it go and continue reading. We can't remember or think of everything, and if you think of all the things you should remember when reading a tale, it will certainly not go well. Inner peace is most important! It's better to do it "wrong," but in a relaxed state and with conviction rather than with obvious stress. It is more important that we give something *positive*, something that is *alive*, than to give it without mistakes. Something that is perfect is not necessarily alive. Rudolf Steiner once told a group of Waldorf school teachers: "A teacher must not be afraid to make mistakes!" This is true for every educator and every parent. If we let the fairy tales be heard, if we tell them, question after question will arise and the advice that we have read or heard will become more and more conscious. We will learn by doing and each time it will just keep getting better and better.

This book is not meant to be a textbook to be worked through before getting to work. I believe that when it comes to fairy tales, it is best to learn while doing. If the words in this book can be a companion on this path of development, I will be very grateful.

## ENDNOTES

1 For more on the role of karma in temperament and life stories, see Udo de Haes, *The Singing, Playing Kindergarten* (WECAN 2015), chapter 5.

2 Avoid allowing children to paint or draw directly after they hear a tale. Listening, especially listening to a fairy tale, requires deep, quiet internalization. This process must have the chance to expand. If a child is asked to act immediately after hearing a story, whether creatively or otherwise, the internalization process is disturbed. The listening experience, which is internally oriented, is asked to become external. It should be clear that this would be confusing and unnatural for the child.

3 My own stories, published in the series *Zonnegeheimen* (*Sun Secrets*) by Vrij Geestesleven, over the years from 1951-1986, were inspired by experiences in schools, and are therefore suitable for school children. They also include some fairy tales and songs appropriate for early childhood groups.

# 6 | Afterword

Interest in fairy tales and their origins has increased in recent decades. More and more people are interested in the so-called "explanations of fairy tales" ("Märchendeutungen"). This is a joyful development, but one that also harbors dangers, especially in the *way* the interest is expressed.

In past centuries, grandmothers usually told fairy tales to young children—older people who had already distanced themselves slightly from worldly materialism and who saw the spiritual world that the child had just left slowly coming closer. These grandmothers were blessed with the ability to give the children, their soul mates, the requests coming from the spiritual world in a living form, through telling fairy tales.

Today such grandmothers are rare. They are just as much in a hurry and just as involved in everyday problems as the rest of us. Contemplation on the end of life, so closely connected with the beginning, is out of fashion, and thus the natural ability to tell fairy tales in later life has been lost.

Instead of the natural connection that used to exist among grandparents, young children, and fairy tales, we now see that both parents and grandparents are interested in studying the backgrounds of the tales. This *could* be productive if learning about the tales meant an *active* search for the *living spirit* of fairy tales, which is the world of the *young child* at the same time. If one's studying is truly a healthy and spirit-driven search, then it will surely guide us to the essence of the young child and her pre-birth origins. This the key to both the soul of the child and the world of fairy tales. Thus, being the grandmother is possible for each and every one of us who sincerely wants it and is willing to follow the path to conquering herself spiritually. Those of us who are not yet able to achieve the level of the grandmother on the physical plane, such as fathers or young playgroup leaders, will find this helpful and comforting. This help is sorely needed because everyone who wants to tell fairy tales will need to learn to become the old grandmother *in their souls.*

However, if adults only want to satisfy their own intellectual and spiritual thirst for knowledge, then nothing of the lost spiritual world will be communicated to the young child when telling a fairy tale; the young child will be given stones instead of bread (see "Dare to make mistakes").

A good example of the above is a scribe. Scribes studied the Holy Scriptures diligently, but at the same time they were the least able to open themselves to the actual life stemming from these spiritual sources.

In the same way, modern interest in fairy tales is in danger of being fixed into a false "spiritual science" about origins, resulting in the dismissal and withering away of the true living heart of the entire world of fairy tales: the essence of the young child.

The adult is robbing the child of the fairy tales in order to satisfy his own spiritual understanding. This seems harsh, but much has already faded away and will continue to do so if we do proceed with care.

There are many good and interesting explanations of fairy tales to be found in the world. They are read and studied by many with great interest. But where is the in-depth study of the fairy tale's greatest task: the development of the young child? Where are we looking to find the true, pre-birth essence of the little child?

I do not want this book to be a collection of fairy tale explanations that adds to "fairy tale science." This book aims to delve deeper into the *living* mystery of the *young child* and her pre-birth origins together with the reader. This path leads us automatically to the world of fairy tales because it expresses this pre-birth mystery of the child. It should therefore also be her daily bread.

We are searching for *the little child* and thus the fairy tales as well, both as *living beings* that are inseparable; born as "twins" who should be raised as one.

If this book has given even the smallest encouragement to this end, then it has achieved its goal.

# About the Author

Daniel Udo de Haes was born in 1899 into a family with six children in Bali, Indonesia (then under Dutch colonial rule). In his ninth year, the family moved to Holland. Daniel studied physics and mathematics at Leiden University and became a teacher in the Hague. He then went to Zeist and encountered the Anthroposophy of Rudolf Steiner, which inspired all his further work.

At a conference he met his future wife, Johanna van Goudover, with whom he had three children. In Zeist, he taught in a Waldorf elementary school, and then worked until his retirement as a teacher in an anthroposophic institute for children with special needs, "Het Zonnehuis."

Toward the end of this period he wrote, illustrated, and self-published a series of books for young children, *Zonnegeheimen*, containing tales, fables and small poems. After his retirement he also wrote a series of educational books for parents and teachers. A focus of his work was the importance of telling the traditional fairy tales to young children. He continued with these educational writings up to his death in March, 1986, in Zeist.

Made in the USA
Columbia, SC
26 June 2018